BEATRICE GIBSON

Deux Soeurs

Bergen Kunsthall
KW Institute of Contemporary Art

Sternberg Press

READER

INTRODUCTION
Axel Wieder

This book accompanies two films and four exhibitions by Beatrice Gibson, which took place at KW Institute for Contemporary Art, Berlin; Camden Art Centre, London; Bergen Kunsthall, and Mercer Union, Toronto. One of the films, *I Hope I'm Loud When I'm Dead,* was co-commissioned as part of the KW Production Series with support from the Julia Stoschek Collection and Outset Germany_Switzerland. The musical score for the other film, *Deux Soeurs Qui Ne Sont Pas Soeurs*, was composed by British composer Laurence Crane and commissioned by Borealis—a festival for experimental music in Bergen, as the first part of the film project. Both films were also shown at numerous festivals, such as Quinzaine (Director's Fortnight), Cannes Film Festival, and the 57th New York Film Festival.

On the one hand, myriad production histories are often a reality of artistic work in film, with projects so extensive in cost and production effort that they exceed the resources available for a single solo exhibition. On the other hand, however, creating connections and working within an expanded network of collaborations is a key conceptual aspect of Beatrice Gibson's artistic methodology. The two films here were made together with the artist's friends and family who were involved on many levels: as actors, writers, musicians, blurring the otherwise strict hierarchies that exist within film production. Born out of an interest in the politics and ethos of experimental music and film, the two new works include sound, text, and images culled from various sources.
The starting point for *Deux Soeurs*, for example, is Gertrude Stein's eponymous script from 1929, written

by Stein as European fascism was building momentum. Gibson's adaptation is set almost a century later in present day Paris and deploys Stein's script as a talismanic guide through a contemporary moment of comparable social and political unrest. *Deux Soeurs* is both a fictional thriller and an act of collective representation and proposes empathy and friendship as a way of dealing with an increasingly turbulent present. The ethos of the film is expressed movingly in a new short text by filmmaker Basma Alsharif, written as a monologue for the project and reprinted here. Similarly, *I Hope I'm Loud When I'm Dead* starts with material shot together with poets CAConrad and Eileen Myles in New York on the eve of the 45th American presidential inauguration in January 2017, and later edited together with words by fellow poets Audre Lorde, Alice Notley, and Adrienne Rich, as well as a soundtrack by Pauline Oliveros. The film ends with a precise remake of the famous final scene from Claire Deni's *Beau Travail* (1999), in which Gibson herself performs, together with her young son, in a touching filmic moment that testifies for care and hope. The films serve as documents of these encounters and confrontations, but in a way also as a reason and a starting point, a medium in which social contexts and ideas become active, and which we are invited to follow on screen.

During the exhibition periods, the collaborative process inherent to the films was expanded through extensive public programs, developed by the artist together with each institution. Many of the film's participants took part in events including talks, workshops, concerts, and screenings that presented a context for Gibson's artistic approach.

This book contains texts and notes which were used in the films, together with material that informed the working process both in its method and direction. Bergen Kunsthall, Camden Art Centre, and Mercer

Union each commissioned a new text by a scholar or writer; respectively Irene Revell, Mason Leaver-Yap, and Erika Balsom. Further texts by some of the participants, such as Eileen Myles and Alice Notley—as well as highly influential contributions by Ursula K. Le Guin, Adrienne Rich, Audre Lorde, and Robert Glück—draw a framework for research into the ethics and politics of friendship.

We thank all contributors to the films and programs and the institutions who worked together on these exhibitions: KW Institute for Contemporary Art, Berlin (Krist Gruijthuijsen, Director; Mason Leaver-Yap, Associate Curator); Camden Art Centre, London (Martin Clark, Director; Sophie Williamson, Exhibitions Curator) and Mercer Union, a centre for contemporary art, Toronto (Julia Paoli, Director and Curator; Aamna Muzaffar, Assistant Curator), together with Bergen Kunsthall and the curatorial team Steinar Sekkingstad, Curator; Maria Rusinovskaya, Curator Live Program; Eva Rowson, Interim Curator Live Program. Thank you especially to KW Institute for Contemporary Art for the support of the publication and all supporters who made this publication possible. We are indebted to the publishers and archives who gave permission to reprint the texts in the reader part of the publication. Sincere thanks to Annette Lux and Lina Grumm (HIT) for accompanying the project in its entirety.

EDGELESSNESS

by Erika Balsom

EDGELESSNESS

Erika Balsom

> I am a galactic cloud so deep
> so involuted that a light wave could take 15
> years to travel through me
> And has
> taken
> I am an instrument in the shape
> of a woman trying to translate pulsations
> into image
> for the relief of the body
> and the reconstruction of the mind.
>
> Adrienne Rich, "Planetarium," 1968

Beatrice Gibson's *I Hope I'm Loud When I'm Dead* (2018) opens with an account of what it is to feel the world coursing through the body—corrosively, brutally. The claustrophobia of crowded underground trains, the shattered windows of urban uprising, the oppressive fear of sudden violence, the dull ache of a warming planet, the fallout of social domination: all push in through chiseled fragments of image and sound, punctuated by blackness. The ideology of neoliberalism preaches a gospel of self-reliance and autonomy, selling to all a retreat from mutual interdependence that benefits only the most privileged few. In the first moments of Gibson's film, the reality of contemporary existence tears through the illusory promises of this paradigm. To live is to be vulnerable, exposed. "I can still feel my body but it's like the skin is gone. It's all nerve, edgeless," the artist relays in voiceover. Forty years after Adrienne Rich described the self as a galactic cloud of deep involution, pressures have intensified. In our cruel and accelerated present, Gibson offers the image of a raw wound through which light waves of actuality pass unimpeded, instantaneously stinging and staining.

Nestled within all these evocations of what denudes the self of epidermal comfort, dissolving by force any sense of bounded individuality, there is something else: glimpses of Gibson's young children, Obie and Laizer. In *I Hope I'm Loud When I'm Dead* and its sororal companion *Deux soeurs qui ne sont pas soeurs* (2019), the bonds of parenthood emerge as a second site at which subjective integrity falters, now not as violence but as ethics. The child is a paragon of an ethical relation to alterity, coming before the self, demanding a relationship to the future in a time of woe, when such a thing can feel so hard to imagine. Here is another edgelessness, very different from the first. These films, more dyad than diptych, with images and themes passing from one to the next and back again, together trace the relationship between these dual dispossessions of the self. They hold the horrors of the world in one hand and the obligation—and joy—of a relation to alterity in the other, searching for reparative responses to the morass of a present ever more privatized, ever more desperate.

In this project of repair, Gibson assigns a central role to queer and feminist poetry. Whether they create literature or cinema, Rich's instruments of translation are still here, shaping the pulsating mess of life into images—not to neutralize or tame the problems of the world but to offer counsels for survival and contestations of what is. *I Hope I'm Loud When I'm Dead* borrows its title from the poet CAConrad. Following the film's opening evocation of crisis, a handheld camera moves around a room in which Gibson and Conrad sit together with curator Mason Leaver-Yap and poet Eileen Myles, all four enveloped in rutilant light. On the soundtrack, United States president Donald Trump speaks of the need to rebuild and restore the promise of America. The irony of this audiovisual counterpoint is palpable; the "we" of Trump's spurious promises excludes those pictured, as it does so many more. Yet the urgency of change is what is at stake for Gibson, too. She excerpts Trump's rebarbative address only to interrupt it with Conrad reading poetry, beginning with the line of the film's title, wresting the mandate of social transformation away from the patriarchal right.

As the presence of Conrad and Myles suggests, these films leave behind the references to male avant-gardists that populate many of Gibson's previous works—be it Cornelius Cardew, William Gaddis, or B.S. Johnson—to espouse a different citational politics, a citational politics *of* difference. *I Hope I'm Loud When I'm Dead* also calls on the poetry of Rich, Audre Lorde, and Alice Notley. These queer and feminist voices mingle with the artist's own, as she embeds them amongst images of daily life: books and toys, tarot cards and crystals, her children at the beach and at home. *Deux soeurs qui ne sont pas soeurs*, meanwhile, is the name of an enigmatic, page-long film scenario written by Gertrude Stein in 1929, until now left unrealized. Gibson begins the film with Notley—a literary granddaughter of Stein[1]—describing her desire to track daily life on multiple levels before delving into a liberal adaptation of Stein's scenario, an oneiric fable of repetition and

1 Notley begins her published lecture "Doctor Williams' Heiresses," quoted by Gibson in *I Hope I'm Loud When I'm Dead*, with an account of artistic parentage that begins with Edgar Allan Poe mating with a goddess. In the messy ancestral lineage she fabulates, she names William Carlos Williams as her grandfather. She states that Williams was married to Stein, but does not name her as grandmother. See: Alice Notley, *Doctor Williams' Heiresses* (Berkeley: Tuumba Press, 1980), np.

recombination in which two women search desperately for a white poodle. To embody Stein's characters, Gibson draws from her community, casting educator Diocouda Diaoune, artist Adam Christensen, curator María Palacios Cruz, and artist-filmmakers Basma Alsharif and Ana Vaz. Collaboration prevails over the mythos of singular authorship, as Gibson moves between her adaptation of Stein's absurdist tale and non-fiction encounters with these friends, several of whom read letters to absent loved ones. All confront unknown prospects: Alsharif and Diaoune, both pregnant, speak to their children in utero, while Vaz questions whether her home country of Brazil, where she no longer lives, has a future. "The barbarism has returned that never went," she says.

Both films pull citation away from its familiar employment as postmodern textual play to render it, as Sara Ahmed has described, a form of feminist memory, a place of feminist dwelling, a way of acknowledging a debt to those who have come before.[2] At the same time, these are works of great intimacy, produced within a cultural moment that sees the first-person singular frequently deployed in art and literature as a guarantee of authenticity—a moral value that is so often a matter of consumption and commodification today. The "I" can be an arrogant dismissal of the "we" that we always are, proclaiming a false uniqueness and autonomy that conforms perfectly to neoliberal demands. By making citation and collaboration integral to these emphatically personal works, Gibson turns away from these tendencies—and the solipsism and narcissism that lurk within them—to see the "I" as an indeterminate

2 Sara Ahmed, *Living a Feminist Life* (Durham: Duke University Press, 2017), 15–16.

field forever shaped and inhabited by others. "This is Alice speaking now …," "This is Audre speaking now …," she says in *I Hope I'm Loud When I'm Dead*, ceding her place to these women. Rather than refer fixedly to a single biography, a single body, as the anchor of meaning and point of focalization, these films embrace the polyvocal weave of the collective. As much as Gibson remains at their core, they are choruses, not monologues, and even less confessions. On this last count, the lodestone of poetry is key: though it may convey what is ownmost, in its judiciousness, it is the antithesis of direct speech, channeling personal expression through the impersonal opacity of crafted language, not to obstruct or dilute, but to intensify. For Gibson and her interlocutors alike, the artifice of rhetoric shapes the miasma of experience into the sharp corners of art.

As with the "I," so with the domain of parenthood: it is an opening onto the outside. The role of the parent is sometimes seen as a retreat from public life, enclosing the child in an impenetrable cocoon. *I Hope I'm Loud When I'm Dead* invokes this shelter, as Gibson cuts between tender images of her partner, Nick Gordon, in a disco-lit bath with their children, and footage of Grenfell Tower burning, with flashes of refugees arriving on a Sicilian beach in between. This constellation stages a candid reckoning with the privilege of private security in the face of endangered, even extinguished, life. Yet understood within the film's larger forcefield, which incessantly situates parenthood in relation to political, ecological, and humanitarian emergency, these cuts figure both as distance *and* relation, irreconcilability *and* proximity. We are not all equally exposed to the gales of precarity, but we are all implicated, and no one is fully exempt from their devastating power. How to cope with the guilt, the responsibility, of relative safety? Perhaps it is a matter of heeding as much as one can from CAConrad's impossible call: "Love all unloved parts without pause."

Gibson suggests that the child is not merely a being requiring protection from a vile world; the child is a being that demands that the parent engage with the world in all its vileness, loving all its unloved parts—because the child is, among other things, a demand for a future that might be different and better than our tumultuous present. This demand shapes *Deux soeurs*, as the two strands of the film—the Stein scenario and the non-fiction testimonies, seemingly so different—are braided together as forms of trans-generational communication, a taking and giving of strength that flows backwards and forwards through time. Both films position parenthood and the citation of women's artistic practices as twin reproductive forces that suture past to future, creating pathways of feminist inheritance. This conception of lineage and responsibility encompasses blood ties but is not bound by them; it is open to creative affinity, exceeding the bounds of heteronormativity and privatized affect. When Diaoune and Alsharif speak to their unborn children, their concerns are both personal and political, whether it involves life as a racialized subject in France or the pain of the Palestinian diaspora. Of her life in Cairo, Alsharif admits, "Our security is precarious here," before adding, "but so is the whole world."

So much is uncertain. But what is certain is that no parent will be able to make a better future for their child alone. The effort of worldmaking is one that we must undertake together, breaking out of secluded enclosures to stand with others. In her engagement with a corpus of queer and feminist cultural production, Gibson suggests that art itself may provide a forum for this experience of transformational collectivity. She, too, reads a letter to her daughter, near the end of *I Hope I'm Loud When I'm Dead*. In it, she describes the film as a resource for resistance to come: "I wanted to put all these voices in one frame for you, so that one day, if needed, you could use them to unwrite whoever it is you're told you're supposed to be." Though it is a gesture of aspiration and empowerment, as well as a statement of confidence in the power of art, it equally harbors a grim acknowledgement: the future might not be any better, any different. Our children, biological or otherwise, could continue to face what we have, or worse. *Deux soeurs* refers less openly to the global political situation than *I Hope I'm Loud When I'm Dead*, but it is a film more palpably under the sign of Saturn, full of somber, seemingly unending nights and plangent music. Danger feels close at hand, because it is. In their mournful song of frustrated desire, does Christensen hurt for the catastrophe that has already occurred or the catastrophe to come? Both films register in their own way the nimbus of anxiety, sadness, and anger that blows in from what Franco "Bifo" Berardi has called the "slow cancellation of the future."

Yet as Antonio Gramsci knew, pessimism of the intellect can be matched by optimism of the will. The letters of *Deux soeurs* voice resilience more than fear, while *I Hope I'm Loud When I'm Dead* concludes with an emphatic assertion of beauty and perseverance via another citation of another woman, as Gibson restages the closing sequence of Claire Denis's *Beau Travail* (1999). In the original, Denis Lavant's character is contemplating suicide when, through the magic of a cut that may also be a leap into the afterlife, Denis delivers him to the dancefloor of the Bar des Alpes. Suspended out of time and freed from the imperial discipline that had governed him, he dances with abandon to the house beat of Corona's "Rhythm of the Night." Cinema resurrects the dead, giving the joy that life could not. Gibson remakes Lavant's solo as a duet with her son, replacing the patriarchal one with the maternal two. The night of dark, collapsed horizons gives way to the night of freedom, play, possibility, togetherness. Through dance, through cinema, through the relationship between mother and child, the world courses through the body once more—again edgeless, now ecstatic.

POE TRY AND DISA STER

by MASON LEAVER-YAP

POETRY AND DISASTER

Mason Leaver-Yap

Who gets to speak of disaster? Who can name it, define its duration, and say when it has come to an end? Breaking news favors the event, the crisis. But what of slow, plural catastrophes, the ones that seem to stretch on without the singularity of a time and a place? In news cycles, there is little drama in the narrative of managed decline, the slow desertion of justice, conflicts that begin and end and blend with others. These things extend beyond the conventionally abridged shock of disaster; their boundaries are more diffuse.

If one can even speak of a "natural" disaster (of which there are few in comparison with its opposite), such a catastrophe can brutally expose pre-existing social and economic rot within sites already so decayed that their messy deficiencies resist the eventfulness of disasters that have been compressed into a name. In such instances, the oft-attendant word "tragedy" can sometimes be deployed immediately after the event to obscure or delay charges of criminality, as if such lamentable and numbing things not yet sheathed in the definition of catastrophe might be fated rather than structured.

Natural or not, the onset of disaster brings about events unlike social life. Declaring a state of emergency enables the triggering of predetermined sets of actions usually hidden from daily operations: rapid response units, exceptional procedures, disaster protocols, emergency powers. These things can be activated by ruling forces that also endow preselected groups with unique and extraordinary abilities to intervene into the democratic order of civil life to use strategies already anticipated for future textbook disasters. In her book *Thinking in an Emergency*

(2012), philosopher Elaine Scarry notes the tendency to create a binary between "acting" and "thinking" in moments of disaster, where acting is immediate, and thinking too slow and ponderous to deal with problems effectively. This binary exists to forestall accountability when things go wrong within a disaster response. "There was not enough time," or, "we had to do something." Of course, in practice, thinking and acting are not so easily disentangled.

When the majority of citizens are disenfranchised from acting (where such activity—or, indeed, inactivity—is the reserve of a ruling power), what of a citizen's thinking, and why is it lesser than acting? Certainly, the denigration of thinking in times of disaster tends to serve a commanding elite and its desire for a single, coherent narrative. But in its fullness, disaster rarely congeals so conveniently, despite attempts to name it otherwise. The poet and philosopher Édouard Glissant has described how the explosive quality of catastrophe—its apparently "momentary" compactness in history (frequently whittled down to encapsulating nouns: Katrina, Hillsborough, Grenfell or simply the word "disaster" itself: Shoah, Al-Nakba)—overwhelms the ability to think of historical precedents, patterns that lead to the present, and possibilities for future resistance. Speaking from the context of the French colonial erasure of Caribbean history, Glissant writes: "Our history emerges at the edge of what we can tolerate, this emergence must be related immediately to the complicated web of events in our past. The past, to which we were subjected, which has not yet emerged as history for us, is, however, obsessively present. The duty of the writer is to explore this obsession, to show its relevance in a continuous fashion to the

1 Édouard Glissant, *Caribbean Discourse: Selected Essays* (Charlottesville/London: University Press of Virginia, 1992), 63.

immediate present."[1] Glissant succinctly points out that disaster is rarely exceptional. With effort and attention, it can be read and written.

Reflecting on 9/11, the earthquake in Haiti, and the aftermath of Hurricane Katrina in her hometown of New Orleans, the poet Nicole Cooley notes that disaster is regularly discussed in terms of "the inability to speak."[2] She counters these assumptions of muteness by instead pointing to ways in which disaster is reproduced through language. Cooley seeks to define a poetry of disaster, the criteria of which include the reliance upon fragments, where the very constitution of broken chronicles performs the disjointed nature of disaster itself. Immediate responses to disaster are always delivered in shards of eyewitness statements, testimonials that seek resonance with others, the partial and the incomplete. Those who gather together these fragmented languages become the interpreters for tangles of time, trauma, and information. Cooley's assessment can be coupled by observations from poet and translator Rob Halpern who describes disaster not only in terms of communal experience but also of absence: "Unlike the death of any one, disaster is what we hold in common as a community, despite its not being here for us to share as a site for communion."[3] Ben Okri also offers a site in his poem "Grenfell Tower, June 2017," a tall stack of compact lines inside the pages of the *Financial Times*; black text in place of a scorched tower: "The voices here must speak for the dead. / Speak for the dead. / Speak for the dead."

2 Nicole Cooley, "Poetry of Disaster," poets.org, 2014, https://poets.org/text/poetry-disaster.
3 Rob Halpern, "Post Disaster," in *Disaster Suites* (Long Beach, CA: Palm Press, 2009), 82.

What are the ethics of distributing languages and openings into the experiences, sufferings, and grief of disaster's survivors? Quoting and paraphrasing a traumatic event—especially others' personal experiences of disaster—has the potential to ventriloquize its harm anew, creating a reductive loop wherein the disaster is simply replayed rather than transformed. Poet and writer Patricia Smith describes the need to ask each time "whether I have the right to enter other lives." Her collection of poems *Blood Dazzler* was inspired by thirty-five elderly residents of St. Rita's Nursing Home in St. Bernard Parish, just outside New Orleans, all of whom died because the facility did not evacuate them before Katrina arrived. "You can either call it exploitation or you can call it witnessing." Becoming a witness for those who had none, Smith points to the thin line between either appropriating violence, or else reimagining it into a strange new form that might offer room for reflection. *Blood Dazzler* purposefully operates in the register of the unfamiliar, embodying disorientation (a defining quality of disaster), and opening in the voice of Katrina herself: "[...] I become / a mouth, thrashing hair, an overdone eye. How dare / the water belittle my thirst, treat me as just / another / small / disturbance, / try to feed me / from the bottom of its hand? / I will require praise, / unbridled winds to define my body, / a crime behind my teeth / because / every woman begins as weather, / sips slow thunder / knows her hips. Every woman / harbours a chaos, can / wait for it, straddling a fever." Smith's Katrina brings to mind the speech of an ancient Sibyl, a woman oracle Heraclitus describes as possessing a "frenzied mouth uttering things not to be laughed at, unadorned and unperfumed, yet reaches through a thousand years with her voice by aid of the god."

The raving oracles—especially women—who anticipate or interpret disaster have traditionally been placed in the genre of myth due to the inconvenience of their voices. The information of sphinxes, sibyls, and witches is pushed into the lyric form—a blend of the fragment, the unfamiliar, and meaning at the edge of what we (choose to) understand. Cassandra, the prophet of disaster to whom no one listened; Iambe, the consoling jester who hanged herself after suffering the disgrace of verbal abuses; Medea, judged as criminal for refusing to maintain the order of the mother and, by extension, the world. These women experience disaster and become it; their truth is made mad, shunned or punished; and their personal disasters are often produced by or result in war. In more recent times, one wonders if much has changed. American poet Muriel Rukeyser wrote in 1968, "I lived in the first century of world wars. / Most mornings I would be more or less insane, / The newspapers would arrive with their careless stories, / The news would pour out of various devices / Interrupted by attempts to sell products to the unseen. / I would call my friends on other devices; / They would be more or less mad for similar reasons. / Slowly I would get to pen and paper, / Make my poems for others unseen and unborn."

Battle cries and poetry can sound the same. Plato was acutely aware of such power when he banished poets—who he described as "the eulogists of tyranny"—from his Republic. "Can poetry mourn in a spirit that does not lead its audience toward the thirst to punish someone?" asks activist and poet Alicia Ostriker. Certainly, thinking and speaking through disaster can be an attempt to articulate a desire for as-yet undelivered justice, and simultaneously be a space for collective grief. Crucially though, this grievance is not procedural, legal, or bureaucratic. It does not speak in the form of the manager; it speaks in the form of the catastrophe. This form, this thinking, has the ability to harness asymmetrical voices into a chorus that argues against the repetition of future disasters. Therein lies the rage and capacity for action. And after action, or indeed through it, the possibility of healing.

"IN PARIS YOU HAVE TO HAVE A FORMULA"

THE CONTROLLED ACCIDENT, FEMINIST PERFORMANCE SCORE(S)

AND GERTRUDE STEIN

BY IRENE REVELL

"IN PARIS YOU HAVE TO HAVE A FORMULA": THE CONTROLLED ACCIDENT, FEMINIST PERFORMANCE SCORE(S) AND GERTRUDE STEIN

Irene Revell

Pauline Oliveros' recorded voice speaks, reverberating across more than fifty years: "But is it music?" An exacting alto softened with familiar Texan warmth, repeated and layered to a point of abstraction that is as much live energetic invocation as hypnotic oblivion. The nine-minute piece is titled *Participle Dangling in Honor of Gertrude Stein*, composed at the University of Toronto Electronic Music Studio in 1966.[1] Oliveros was by no means the first of her generation to lionize Stein, nor even the first composer. For another favorite example, Earle Brown had insisted several years earlier that "Gertrude Stein said many things when you come to think about it for a few minutes (and I suggest 183, 765, 432, 109 minutes for a starter)."[2] This passion was fed from within the heart of the New York Fluxus community by Dick Higgins' re-publishing of a series of Stein's writings: *The Making of Americans* (1966), *Geography and Plays* (1968), *Lady Church Amiably* (1969), *Matisse, Picasso and Gertrude Stein* (1972), *A Book Concluding with As A Wife Has A Cow* (1973), *How To Write* (1973).

1 See Pauline Oliveros, "'Participle Dangling in Honor of Gertrude Stein': Composing with Hugh Le Caine's Special Purpose Tape Recorder at UTEMS in 1966," *eContact! Online Journal for Electroacoustic Practices* 17.2 (Montréal: The Canadian Electroacoustic Community, January 2016), https://econtact.ca/17_2/oliveros_lecaine.html.

2 Earle Brown, "Planned Panichood," in *An Anthology of Chance Operations*, ed. Jackson Mac Low and La Monte Young (New York: George Maciunas & Jackson Mac Low, 1963), 22.

In Higgins' Something Else Press newsletter of September 1972 he would ask: "Why do we publish so much Gertrude Stein?"[3] A question rendered effectively rhetorical, in spite of his ensuing tract, by its alternative answer in emphatically oversized typeface on the adjacent page: "WHY NOT!?" Whilst Oliveros' question is equally rhetorical, a parody of the unending populist ridicule of contemporary arts—and the reference to Stein intended most in relation to the repetition of the tape—this text concerns itself with two arising questions: But is it a *feminist* music? And more specifically, what does Stein have to do with it? Two questions that might emerge over the following years of Oliveros' work and that of some of her immediate peers, and which may be as much at stake in the two new film works presented in this publication.

Control and Accident

Beatrice Gibson and I share an ongoing conversation that evolves out of our mutual interests in the score-based performance works of this period. Works that emerge in the wake of John Cage's 1952 composition *4'33"* and the closely related birth of the *event score* in Fluxus amidst a wider opening out of possibilities.[4] Works that seek a "difference" in each new iteration as opposed to the relative fidelity to the "original" commanded by conventional musical scores. Per-

3 Dick Higgins, "Why do we publish so much Gertrude Stein," The Something Else Newsletter September 1972, http://primaryinformation.org/oldsite/SEP/Something-Else-Press_Newsletter_V2N4.pdf.

4 For a full account see Liz Kotz, *Words to Be Looked At: Language in 1960s Art* (Cambridge, MA: MIT Press, 2007).

formance scores that employ more accessible, non-musical forms of notation, often textual, instructional. That are "intermedia" or make use of life itself as their medium, often requiring no traditional performance skills, musical or otherwise. Some have previously formed crucial material in Gibson's films such as the work of Cornelius Cardew and event scores by George Maciunas, Mieko Shiomi, and others.[5] Moreover, I am fascinated by the mode of thinking that draws these kinds of formal structures into an expanded approach to filmmaking, the process of filmmaking itself as a "score-like" form of production.[6] Here I am particularly compelled by Gibson's interlinked appeal to Maya Deren and her notion of the *controlled accident* in regard to these questions.

By 'controlled accident' I mean the maintenance of a delicate balance between what is there spontaneously and naturally as evidence of the independent life of actuality and the persons and activities that are independently introduced into the scene.[7]

Gibson expands on the *controlled accident* in her own works to understand "how key compositional parameters are decided on during a production process [...] The film is a result of a set of decisions that are left to unfold on their own terms, just one

5 Beatrice Gibson's film *The Tiger's Mind* (2012) is based on Cardew's eponymous score. Her films *Solo for Rich Man* (2015) and *Crippled Symmetries* (2015) work with event scores by Maciunas, Shiomi, and others.

6 This is a notion that may be loosely in common with other peers and friends. Notable here is the work of Pauline Boudry/Renate Lorenz, including their two films that are dedicated to Oliveros' scores, *To Valerie Solanas and Marilyn Monroe in Recognition of their Desperation* (2013) and *Telepathic Improvisation* (2017).

7 Maya Deren, "Cinematography: The Creative Use of Reality," in *The Avant-Garde Film: A Reader of Theory and Criticism*, ed. P. Adams Sitney (New York: Anthology of Film Archives, 1960/1978), 66.

possible iteration of a set of production parameters."[8]

Whilst neither anachronistic nor without proximities, Deren, now more readily associated with early experimental feminist cinema, here poses an unlikely yet generative line of thought, refracted back through the confluence of Gibson's mutual interest. What is at stake in such a medial transposition, the performed score as *controlled accident*? Deren offers an incisive articulation of the interconnected duality of such works, the "controlled" and the "accident." The absolute authority of the score, its instructions, its singular author, and the shifting or sharing in performance, here given over to the determination of the performer, *the other*, and chance itself. That this shoot, this performance is only one in any number of possible iterations, yet one with a deeply rooted sense of specificity and (socio-political) context. This is something intrinsic to score-based works such as *4'33"*, yet which is often overlooked in their discussion.[9]

Beatrice Gibson's new film works start out with a set of determined parameters—their scores. And both develop their own internal logic accordingly, through this sharing of authority. *I Hope I'm Loud When I'm Dead* (2018) initiates with an invitation to one poet who invites a second; a film that comes to double back on its spine, to speak of reproduction and death, contorting and liberating in its final dance. The second, *Deux soeurs qui ne sont pas soeurs* (*Two Sisters Who Are Not Sisters*, 2019), with its underpinnings in Stein's eponymous script, might be

8 See my essay "Striking Coins" for Gibson's exhibition "Crippled Symmetries" (Collective Gallery, Edinburgh, 2015).
9 For an enlightening discussion of socio-political context in this work see Philip Gentry, "The Cultural Politics of *4'33"*: Identity and Sexuality," in *Tacet* 1 (Dijon: Les presses du reel, 2012).

understood as a more conventional kind of score. Nevertheless, one that produces difference through its live realization; just as much a set of parameters to unfold with specific serendipities and demands, new connections, new locations.

The Feminist Performance Score

Compounding on Deren, I am invested in the thinking through of the potential for such scores—already understood as radical in various other senses—to offer a feminist aesthetic. My notion of a *feminist performance score* finds its genesis in Oliveros' 1970 work *To Valerie Solanas and Marilyn Monroe in Recognition of their Desperation*. The late 1960s saw a shift in Oliveros' thinking, leaving behind the San Francisco Tape Music Center, of which she was a co-founder, to set up the Music Department at UC San Diego within a forested cliff-top utopia of brutalist concrete and beaches stretching to infinity. A move away from the technology of tape and towards the composition of textual scores for group situations. An emphasis on consciousness, improvisation, and listening—"listening to long tones and listening to the environment"[10]—with a growing affinity for the nascent US Women's Movement. A consolidation of these shifting interests, *To Valerie Solanas and Marilyn Monroe in Recognition of their Desperation* is a two-page score of dense textual instructions that draws on a section of Valerie Solanas' SCUM Manifesto on the relationship between the individual and the group. That is to say that each performer

10 Moira Roth, "An Interview with Pauline Oliveros," in *New Performance* 1, no. 2 (1977): 41–51.

follows an identical score and chooses five tones of their own, kept to themselves prior to performance, but later shared in a dynamic whose primary focus is on group listening.[11] The work constitutes a perfect expression of the dual needs for autonomy and community at stake in political and other forms of organization. Long discordant tones in a complex interplay: a contemplative drone that befits the double dedication of the piece, Monroe and Solanas, *I hope I'm loud when I'm dead.*

As such, this work seems to emphatically suggest itself as a *feminist* performance score, explicitly in form and content, title and structure, and was to be shortly followed by Oliveros' *Sonic Meditations*, brief textual scores developed with her Women's Ensemble group at UC San Diego.[12] It seems no coincidence that this score-based format was taken up in these various feminist expressions. The performance score as an exacting, two-dimensional visual or textual form on the one hand, and an anarchic state of indeterminate, iterative live-ness on the other. A doubling, a multiplying. A clear, single author on the page but a more complex shifting or sharing of authority in performance, with accordingly distributed forms of labor. A piece of paper that can be easily copied and transmitted with profuse uncontainable outcomes. A document with authority that can stand in for a multitude of moments that have and will come to pass. Whilst feminist movement(s) have struggled with bridging the need for the autonomy of singular voices and the desire for collectivity in its inevitable mess, the performance

11 Roth, "An Interview with," 41–51.
12 For an extended discussion of Oliveros' *Sonic Meditations* and related feminist activities, see Martha Mockus, *Sounding Out: Pauline Oliveros and Lesbian Musicality* (London: Routledge, 2005).

score seems almost the perfect emblem. Manifesto-like in its written authority, a discrete stand-in for the complexity of collaboration.

The publication *Womens Work* (1975–8) is a collection of performance scores in two issues that are multi-disciplinary, textual, and instructional. Self-published in New York City by Fluxus artist Alison Knowles and composer Annea Lockwood, the collection includes Oliveros amongst its twenty-five contributors.[13] The very existence of such a collection seems to give further traction to the notion of a feminist performance score, confirming not only that there are these further examples, but moreover, that the performance score was a medium chosen for the expression of a feminist project in this context.[14] The collection poses at once a *feminist* challenge to the preceding overwhelmingly male history of the post-Cagean performance score, as much as posing a *formal* challenge to the history of the feminist art movement that tended to focus on gallery-based media. Rather, the collection hosts a diversity of practices that include composition, choreography, fine art performance, video art, painting, and astrology. Amongst other diverse facets, ages range from Beth Anderson in her twenties to Sari Dienes in her seventies—an expression of the significance of inter-generational dialogue and collaboration within these communities. *Participle Dangling in Honor of Gertrude*

13 I have also discussed *Womens Work* in the publication *ORGASMIC STREAMING ORGANIC GARDENING ELECTRO-CULTURE* that accompanied the exhibition project of the same name, co-curated with Karen Di Franco at Chelsea Space, London, 2018.

14 A longer discussion of the *feminist performance score* appears in my essay “Introducing *Womens Work*: Exploring the Feminist Performance Score” in the forthcoming anthology *Performing Indeterminacy* (Cambridge University Press).

Stein (1966), *The Pathways of the Grandmothers* (1978), *MMM, A lullaby for Daisy Pauline* (1980), *Crone Music* (1990).[15]

Most significantly within the group, there is a range of relationships to feminist and other politics. In the first instance, whilst some of the scores were written for the collection, others had circulated for a decade or more, in different live and published contexts, and indeed would go on to do so afterwards. Hence the collection is as much an act of framing and contextualization as any kind of harmonizing of practices a statement that these works can co-exist together in this feminist dicussion as much as in their other contexts. As Lockwood puts it, "the intention was to assert that there were many women doing really good work whose names should be more and more familiar,"[16] supplemented by Knowles' assertion that "choices [were] based wholly on the quality and strength of the work."[17] I would assert that the clearest expression of any shared feminist praxis amongst the contributors comes in the sublimated form of the collection itself, with its explicit feminist framing. And as a collection, its capacity to play host to this diversity—not a generic, flattened participation but assertive convictions, a politics of citation. A politics of citation that becomes embodied in its physical hosting: hosted within the printed pages of the collection, and hosting to come in its invitation to perform, its live moments.

15 All work titles by Pauline Oliveros.
16 Annea Lockwood in an interview with me, "You look at a score, you do it," *Cesura//Acceso* 2 (January 2017), 118–27.
17 Letter from Alison Knowles to Jean Brown, undated, Jean Brown Papers, Box 28, Folder 36 (The Getty Research Institute, Special Collections, Los Angeles).

Stein's Salon Expanded

If the speculative *feminist performance score(s)* exist in this locus subtended by Oliveros' work of the early 1970s and the further act of collecting that constitutes *Womens Work*, they are at the heart of a modest snowballing of related activity, within and beyond score-based works. I'd like to end by focusing on one such activity, drawing further on this notion of "hosting," and returning us to Stein. Over New Year's Eve of 1974/75, and on the cusp of compiling the first issue of *Womens Work*, Alison Knowles and Annea Lockwood, together with Jean Rigg, manager of the Merce Cunningham Dance Company, would together organize a fifty-hour "marathon reading" of Gertrude Stein's *The Making of Americans*.[18] It was to become an annual tradition: "[I]ncreasingly large groups of well-known artists, unknown artists, Stein fans, SoHo residents, and passersby [would] come together to pass the New Year by listening to and reading this 925 page book," explains composer Tom Johnson in his description published in the 1977/78 edition of *The Village Voice*, which by this point had relocated from Artists Space to Paula Cooper Gallery where it would continue into the 1980s.[19] Although the project derives from the writings of Stein, static on the page, Johnson describes it in the same breath as Knowles' own propositional and event scores, "concerned

18 Emmett Williams elucidates that the format was borrowed from a project with his students. See Emmett Williams, "My Life in Flux," in *The Last Art College: Nova Scotia College of Art and Design, 1968–1978*, ed. Garry Neill Kennedy (Cambridge, MA: MIT Press, 2012).
19 Tom Johnson, *The Voice of New Music* (Paris: Editions 75, 1989), 316–17.

with social situations [...] bringing people together."[20] More recently, Annea Lockwood summarized her reflections:

It was like a great encampment, people drifted in and out. With kids, without kids. We got really tired, we got punch drunk. It was a great challenge to read late and keep one's tongue from getting twisted around Steinian configurations [...] There's no way to over-emphasize how important we all were to each other, many of us knowing many of us, and not necessarily directly collaborating but frequently falling into collaboration. There's no way to over-emphasize how thrilling that environment, that soup of artists was to me. It was a most hopeful way to usher in a New Year.[21]

Both descriptions inevitably recall Stein's own Paris salon. "[I]n Paris you have to have a formula," Stein explains through the doubled voice of Alice B. Toklas.[22] Avowing that there is a loose rule about who may be admitted—"everybody was supposed to be able to mention the name of someone who had told them about it"—but one that in effect admits anyone willing to adhere. In 1970s New York, in this more public situation, there is a different formula with its own logic: the hosts are clearly named, as are a number of pre-determined readers, yet surely these were to swell and shift as the hours unfolded, the same and different each further year. And while the hosts are demarcated as the authors that set the thing in motion, the nature of the "marathon" here only

20 Ideas taken further in relation to Knowles' practice in Nicole L. Woods, "Object/Poem: Alison Knowles' Feminist Archite(x)ture," *X-tra* 15, no. 1 (Fall 2012).
21 Annea Lockwood in an interview with the author, 2018, unpublished.
22 Gertrude Stein, *The Autobiography of Alice B. Toklas* (London: The Bodley Head, 1933), 14.

makes all the more explicit that such works need to open out to others, that they require others to distribute their labor.

Stein here casts a figure of the host that is always a doubling, a doubling troubled, as in *Deux soeurs qui ne sont pas soeurs*. Radical sameness.[23] The generative discomfort produced by familial affiliations, love and friendships, horizontal, multiple, that do not serve the normative reproductive matrix. A child costumed in a nightclub leading the dance. A feminism where children are not so much a subject matter but participants, performers on equal terms. Reproductive labor in its expanded sense that also produces performance, film, community, "that soup." The *feminist performance score*: a structure that may host collaborators, friends, lovers, children in performance, that expands across these activities. And in this contemporary instance, two films that are exactly such hosting structures, that bleed into each other, expand into an exhibition, and the many live contributions that constituted the series of solo exhibitions that featured Beatrice Gibson's new films, "Crone Music" (Camden Art Centre, London), "I Couldn't Sleep in My Dream" (Bergen Kunsthall), and "Plural Dreams of Social Life" (Mercer Union, Toronto), all 2019.

23 "Radical sameness" is a term coined in the eponymous self-published 2012 zine by Rudy Can't Fail.

I HOPE I'M LOUD WHEN I'M DEAD • 2018

DEUX SOEURS QUI NE SONT PAS SOEURS • 2019

FILM,

DEUX SOEURS QUI NE SONT PAS SOEURS (1928)

FILM, TWO SISTERS WHO ARE NOT SISTERS (1928)

by GERTRUDE STEIN

FILM, TWO SISTERS WHO ARE NOT SISTERS
Gertrude Stein

Around the corner from a boulevard outside of Paris a washerwoman of a certain age with a bundle of laundry that she is busy delivering pauses to pick up a photograph of two white poodles, at which she gazes intently. A two-seater automobile is parking at the curb. All of a sudden, two ladies get out of the car and rush over to the washerwoman and ask to see the photograph. She shows them and the two ladies are full of admiration for the photo until a young woman who is made up as though she has just won a prize in a beauty pageant and then got herself lost on the street, walks by, notices the empty car, scurries into it and begins to cry. At this moment, the two ladies get back into the car and throw the young woman out. She stumbles into the washerwoman, who begins questioning her, and the car is driven off by the two ladies, and suddenly the washerwoman realizes that her photo is missing. She spots a young man and immediately begins telling him what has happened.

A few hours later, in front of an employment agency on rue du Dragon, there is another, younger washerwoman with a bundle of laundry. The car belonging to the two ladies drives up, stops and the two ladies get out and show the washerwoman the photo of the two white poodles. The washerwoman looks at it with pleasure and excitement, but that is all. At this very moment the beauty queen walks up, cries for joy and hurries over to the car. As the two ladies get back into their car they drop a parcel, but they still have the photo and they drive off quickly.

Two days later, the first washerwoman is back on her street with a bundle of laundry and she notices the beauty queen walking up with a parcel in her hand.

And at the same time she sees the young man. Then all three of them are together and suddenly the car drives by with the two ladies, and with them is a real live white poodle, and in the poodle's mouth is a parcel. The washerwoman, the beauty queen and the young man watch the dog go by and they understand nothing.

FILM, DEUX SOEURS QUI NE SONT PAS SOEURS
Gertrude Stein

Au coin d'une rue d'un boulevard extérieur de Paris une blanchisseuse d'un certain âge avec son paquet de linge qu'elle était en train de livrer, s'arrête pour prendre dans ses mains et regarder la photo de deux caniches blancs et elle la regarde avec ardeur. Une automobile de deux places stationnait le long du trottoir. Tout à coup, deux dames en descendent et se précipitent sur la blanchisseuse en demandant à voir la photo. Elle la fait voir et les deux dames sont pleines d'admiration jusqu'au moment où une jeune femme qui est coiffée comme si elle venait d'avoir un prix au concours de beauté et après s'être égarée dans la rue, passe et à ce moment voit l'auto vide, se dépêche d'entrer et se met à pleurer. A ce moment, les deux dames entrent dans l'auto et jettent la jeune femme dehors. Elle tombe contre la blanchisseuse qui commence à la questionner, et l'auto conduite par les deux dames part, et tout à coup la blanchisseuse voit qu'elle n'a plus sa photo. Elle voit un jeune homme et elle lui raconte tout de suite l'histoire.

Quelques heures plus tard, devant un bureau de placement, rue du Dragon, il y a une autre blanchisseuse plus jeune avec son paquet de linge. La voiture des deux dames approche, s'arrête, et les deux dames descendent et font voir à la blanchisseuse la photo des deux caniches blancs. Elle regarde avec plaisir et excitation, mais c'est tout. Juste à ce moment la jeune femme du prix de beauté approche pousse un cri de joie et se précipite vers la voiture. Les deux dames entrent dans leur auto et, en entrant, laissent tomber un petit paquet, mais toujours elles sont en possession de la photo et elles partent précipitamment.

Le surlendemain la première blanchisseuse est encore dans sa rue avec son paquet de linge et elle voit la jeune femme du prix de beauté approcher avec un petit paquet à la main. Et en même temps elle voit le jeune homme. Ils sont tous les trois alors ensemble et tout à coup elle passe, l'auto, avec les deux dames et il y a avec elles un vrai caniche blanc et dans la bouche du caniche est un petit paquet. Les trois sur le trottoir le regardent passer et n'y comprennent rien.

Our Security is Precarious Here

by BASMA ALSHARIF

NOTRE SÉCURITÉ EST PRÉCAIRE ICI

OUR SECURITY IS PRECARIOUS HERE

Basma Alsharif

I think I've imagined it at various instances in my life. This thing, that would be made of me, but completely alien. I imagined it as a full-grown adult, as a toddler, as an infant.

In reality, I made mistakes I took careless risks and then started to wonder if my body wanted or could take this on. It seemed impossible. Like deciding that one day I would learn to fly with the same arms that I'd always had.

I remember one of my gynecologists telling me once, in a very medical and non-mystical sort of way, that the body will sometimes choose not to ovulate, the egg will refuse to descend in order to prevent the possibility of fertilization because it knows the body is in a less than ideal situation for hosting.

This of course is not usually the case as women conceive all the time who are completely unfit or live in violent or unstable environments. I myself live in the most fertile continent on the planet. In an over-populated, polluted, and fascist city. But I have no other home. No original place where I am from. I never did and never will.

Today, in an attempt to be hypnotized, I was asked to imagine a field and at the end of it a gate. Which I did, because it exists: in Gaza. Or at least, it did. What the hypnotist was telling me to do was what I had already done, in real life, with a camera. A small rickety Super 8 film camera.

The sun was shining on the field and I could no longer remember who was with me there that day, but I wasn't alone, because there was the shadow of a person to my right. Later I would hypnotize myself into that same field from other places and walk around, making sure it wouldn't disappear, allowing others the possibility of visiting it through me.

Today, I could see it, but it was only the image of that field. The Super 8 image of it because that place has disappeared—as it has, willfully, since I was born.

Today my home is the nape of the neck of a human being who is also from nowhere, for different reasons. We both know that we could have slipped between each other's fingers. That if we hadn't met again. That if we hadn't written or insisted, if we hadn't fought for each other despite fear and distance, that we would still be searching for a home, without realizing it. And without trying, in fact, while trying to avoid it, you came to be. You forced your way despite everything. And we could still lose you. Before and after you are born. But today, while holding you, I realized as I stepped off the last step I was being instructed off of, the step that would lead to my safe space where I could hold you I realized that there was nothing beyond the step, it was black, like the fluid that surrounds you when we get to peek at you every so often, so when I was told to reach out and carry you in my arms, to hold you in this special safe place of ours, I realized that we were holding each other inside of my uterus, and the two of us there together, being held by Philipe, inside of the void you insisted on making your home in, despite our hesitations, our fears, our turmoil. Despite how little we know about what to do with you, how to prepare for you. Despite that we speak four broken languages between the two of us. Our security is precarious here, but so is the whole world.

NOTRE SÉCURITÉ EST PRÉCAIRE ICI
Basma Alsharif

Je pense que j'ai imaginé dans des moments divers de ma vie. Cette chose, qui serait faite de moi, mais complètement étranger. Je l'imaginais comme un adulte, un bambin, un nourrisson.

En réalité, j'ai commis des erreurs, pris des risques négligents, puis commencé à me demander si mon corps le voulait ou pouvait le supporter. Cela semblait impossible. C'est comme décider qu'un jour j'apprendrais à voler avec les mêmes bras que j'avais toujours eu.

Je me souviens que l'un de mes gynécologues m'avait dit une fois, d'une manière très médicale et non mystique, que le corps choisirait parfois de ne pas ovuler, l'ovule refuserait de descendre pour éviter la possibilité d'une fécondation car il connaissait que le corps est dans une situation moins qu'idéale pour l'hébergement.

Ceci, bien sûr, n'est généralement pas le cas, car les femmes concevoir tout le temps, qui sont totalement inapte ou qui vivent dans des environnements violents ou instables. Je vis moi-même sur le continent le plus fertile de la planète. Dans une ville surpeuplée, polluée et fasciste. Mais je n'ai pas d'autre endroit. Pas de lieu d'origine d'où je viens. Je n'ai jamais eu et je n'aurais jamais.

Aujourd'hui, dans une tentative d'être hypnotise, l'hypnotiseur m'a demandé d'imaginer un champ et au bout de celui-ci une porte. Ce que j'ai fait, car il existe: à Gaza. Ou du moins, il existait. Ce que l'hypnotiseur me disait de faire, c'est ce que j'avais déjà fait, dans la vie réelle, avec une caméra. Un petit camera super 8mm.

Le soleil brillait sur le champ et je ne pouvais

plus me rappeler qui était avec moi ce jour-là, mais je n'étais pas seul, parce qu'il y avait l'ombre d'une personne sur ma droite. Plus tard, je m'hypnotisais dans ce même domaine depuis d'autres endroits et me promenais, en m'assurant qu'il ne disparaîtrait pas, laissant la possibilité aux autres de le visiter à travers moi.

Aujourd'hui, je pouvais le voir, mais ce n'était que l'image de ce champ. L'image en super 8 mm parce que cet endroit a disparu—comme il l'a fait volontairement depuis ma naissance.

Aujourd'hui, ma maison est la nuque d'un être humain qui vient aussi de nulle part, pour des raisons différentes. Nous savons tous les deux que nous aurions pu nous glisser entre les doigts. Que si nous n'étions pas revus. Que si nous n'avions pas écrit ou insisté, si nous n'avions pas combattu l'un pour l'autre malgré la peur et la distance, nous serions toujours en train de chercher une maison sans nous en rendre compte. Et sans essayer, en fait, en essayant de l'éviter, vous êtes venu à être. Vous avez forcé votre chemin malgré tout. Et nous pourrions encore vous perdre. Avant et après votre naissance. mais aujourd'hui, en te tenant, j'ai réalisé, en descendant de la dernière marche, on m'informait de descendre, le marché qui mènerait à mon espace de sécurité où je pourrais te tenir, j'ai réalisé qu'il n'y avait rien au-delà de la marche, elle était noire, comme le liquide qui vous entoure quand nous avons le temps de vous aperçu de temps en temps, alors quand on m'a dit de te tendre la main et de te porter dans mes bras, de te tenir dans notre endroit sûr, j'ai réalisé que nous nous tenions l'un l'autre dans mon utérus, et nous deux ensemble, tenus par Philipe, à l'intérieur du vide que tu avais insisté de s'installer, malgré nos hésitations, malgré nos peurs, nos tourmente. Malgré le peu de choses que nous savons sur ce qu'il faut faire avec toi, comment se préparer pour toi. Malgré que nous parlions quatre langues cassées entre nous deux. Notre sécurité est précaire ici, de même que le monde entier.

LOUD, DEAD

Script Notes
by BEATRICE GIBSON

LOUD, DEAD: SCRIPT NOTES
Beatrice Gibson

VOICE

I'm in the underground heading towards Oxford Circus. It's about 6pm. It's packed. The train stops suddenly in a tunnel. Bodies twitch. A fist clenches in my throat. I can still feel my body except it's like the skin has gone. It's all nerve. Edgeless. Pulsating. There's intense breathlessness. The blood is thumping. It's like being in a club. I feel weightless. Unstitched. I feel chewed apart.

VOICE

What are you afraid of?

VOICE

I'm afraid of my anger, afraid it will get inside them.

I'm afraid of sheer unsteadiness, of night time crisis as tone.

VOICE

This is Alice speaking now: *it's not my consciousness.*

I study but my physiology. My blood and my breathing, my vision, my walk, the chapping of my lips, the greying of my hair etc. Dirty jokes, a tiny car drives down my neck and over my shoulder.

VOICE

One night I dream the little Japanese erasers in the shape of french desserts that litter the house are dipped in a powder that makes them grow to the size of buildings. Cream pushes through window panes. Everything is white, sugary, snow like. I can't breathe.

VOICE

This is Audre speaking now: *I am inside the shadow dipped upon your horizon. I have no sister no mother no children left, only a tideless ocean of moonlit women.*

VOICE

This is Adrienne speaking now: *A woman in the shape of a monster, a monster in the shape of a woman the skies are full of them. Galaxies of women, there doing penance for impetuousness, ribs chilled.*

Dear Laizer

When I was filled up with you, I felt heavy with responsibility. Your half-formed limbs pushing against the edges of me. I wanted to put all these voices in one frame for you, so that one day if needed, you could use them to un-write whoever it is you're told you're supposed to be.

Sometimes you are so alien to me; your dark brown eyes, your tiny legs, one crossed over the other, in the sand. I want to say this one thing just for you. Grief, war, destruction, fear, it's almost all okay because these voices exist.

The person who teaches me the most is you. Your jammy, buttery fingers as they pull me away from my desk. Because of you I am tone of voice, all nerve, edgeless and pulsating. I can breathe.

(SOMA)TIC POETRY RITUAL

& Resulting Poem
by CACONRAD

(SOMA)TIC POETRY RITUAL & RESULTING POEM
CAConrad

M.I.A. ESCALATOR

for Jen Benka & Carol Mirakove

I rode several of my favorite escalators in Philadelphia, taking notes up and down the vantages. At the top and bottom of the ride I would show photographs of myself to strangers and ask, "EXCUSE ME, have you seen this person?" Sometimes there was confusion, "ISN'T THAT YOU?" I would reply, "No, many people think I look like HER, but have you seen HER?" I feel very fortunate to have been born BEFORE the ultrasound machine. My generation was the last generation to have a male and female name waiting at the other end of the birth canal. My generation is the last to have our mothers touch their bellies talking to us as male and female. Pink or blue?

Both pink and blue, "Have you seen this person?" I enjoyed my conversations with strangers and made at least one new friend, a handsome man who knew I was the person in the photograph. That person, I am that person and agreed. The ultrasound machine gives the parents the ability to talk to the unborn by their gender, taking the intersexed nine-month conversation away from the child. The opportunities limit us in our new world. Encourage parents to not know, encourage parents to allow anticipation on either end. Escalators are a nice ride, slowly rising and falling, writing while riding, notes for the poem, meeting new people at either end, "Excuse me, EXCUSE ME …" My escalator notes became a poem.

I HOPE I'M LOUD WHEN I'M DEAD

I have a
mannequin for
a paperweight
it is difficult to
type with such a
large paperweight
I reach around
lovers late into
night typing
from behind it is
impossible to
tell which
is Virgil
poetry
can be
of use
the field of flying
bullets the hand
reaches through
loving the aftertaste
finding a deeper
third taste
many are
haunted by
human cruelty through
the centuries
I am haunted by
our actions since
breakfast
you said *too much poetry*
I said *too much war*
the biggest mistake for
love is straining
there was a
door marked
MISTAKE we
entered
you said *too much fooling around*
I said *fuck off and die*

MY BOX

EILEEN MYLES

MY BOX

Eileen Myles

in terms of
design one
box is colored
orange

the one you wanted
always is and
sits in the bathroom
of anyone's
house cause
that's what
she wants
it's choosing
that wakes things
up

I wondered how
long all
that I needed and encountered
here
would come like a wave
not the shake
but the after
effects
and this box
did say
there was a way
to see this
thing
a-
lone

July called
it calculus
what is
comes in boxes
what is not
comes in waves
the dots
between

mountains
surround us
and I say
they are more
marvelous than
the sea

way overhead

I like flying over
them too
thinking
that is home
these crazy bumps
when we drive
into them
tomorrow
it won't be bam
it means up
swirling on the
edge of a
cup and if you
don't watch
me like a
hawk I won't
be scared
I want to be
loved like
a sunbeam

that is
it comes
across the room
or the ocean
you know the
way I drive
I want to lift
your fear
like a bonnet
and kiss
your living
face. Here
this is
mine. Don't
misunderstand
me.

AMARETTO TO TASTE

ADAM CHRISTENSEN

AMARETTO TO TASTE

Adam Christensen

My youngest nephew carried a dead shrew by the tail. He put it in the box with the other one. The neighbor's cat on a rampage. In between killings she'd shat in the sandpit. Small narratives were drawn on the box before we buried it in the driveway. We stuck a flower in the fresh soil. My sister was making jam with the plums we'd plucked earlier.

Pour 200ml water and 600g sugar in a pot with 1kg halved plums. Add a cinnamon stick. Let it absorb for two hours. Stir occasionally. Parboil while stirring. When the sugar has melted boil for another ten minutes until the plums are tender. Keep stirring. Carefully remove the plums with a spoon. Put them in scalded jars rinsed with Atamon. Boil the jam until sticky. Skim the pickle. Add Amaretto and Atamon to taste. Pour the jam over the plums. Cool down before sealing.

Served with homemade vanilla ice cream.
I went to bed early. One of the boys screamed out in a nightmare. No no no! I must do my spelling!
I woke up before dawn. Caught the train north. Boarded the ferry. Seagulls hovering above. Guiding the boat towards Göteborg. One of the birds flew near. Sharp-eyed. Glancing at my sister's homemade knækbrød in my hand. I wasn't prepared to share. The seagulls returned to Danish shores. Cliffs rose out of the waves. Yellow graffiti painted on one. I was picked up by a Bentley. Cream leather seats. Had a nap. Some strong coffee. Licorice.
I drew black lines down my arms. Black circles on my shoulder. Red circles on my chest. Stepped into my shiny blue high heels. I entered through the black backdrop. I crossed the empty stage.

Stepped into a red spotlight. I jerked my body to the cadenced rhythm. I dropped to the floor. Lights on. I staggered off. Tall monochrome towers came crashing towards me. I slipped past them. Backstage. Another coffee. Cue. Back in the red light. Knocking-off time. A shower. A shave. Free sparkles. A tongue licked the soles of my heels. Two women in bodysuits guarding the entrance. One of them had orange eyes. Synchronized dancing. A cigar. French kisses with three boys. French. Columbian. Polish. A smack on the bum. Afterparty on a roof terrace. I followed Jackie Turner and the girl with orange eyes further up a ladder. We sat on the roof's apex away from everyone else. Panoramic view of the city. She leaned forward to kiss us both. Her clip-on ponytail fell off. It slid down the steep roof. Fell off the edge. Landed in a shrieking girl's cocktail. She started crying. Her boyfriend drew a knife and threw it in the air. I caught it between my teeth. Threw it right back. Sudden death. I woke up in jail. Jackie Turner bailed me out. We took the tram. End station. Climbed the rocks. Dived naked into the cold sea. Swam with a jellyfish. Packed my suitcase. Stole liquid eyeliner at the airport. Jumped the plane to Praha with an Oslo detour. Saw the tiny wheel under the wing touch-down. Skid marks and a puff of smoke.

SELECTED FILM STILLS

I HOPE I'M LOUD WHEN I'M DEAD (2018)

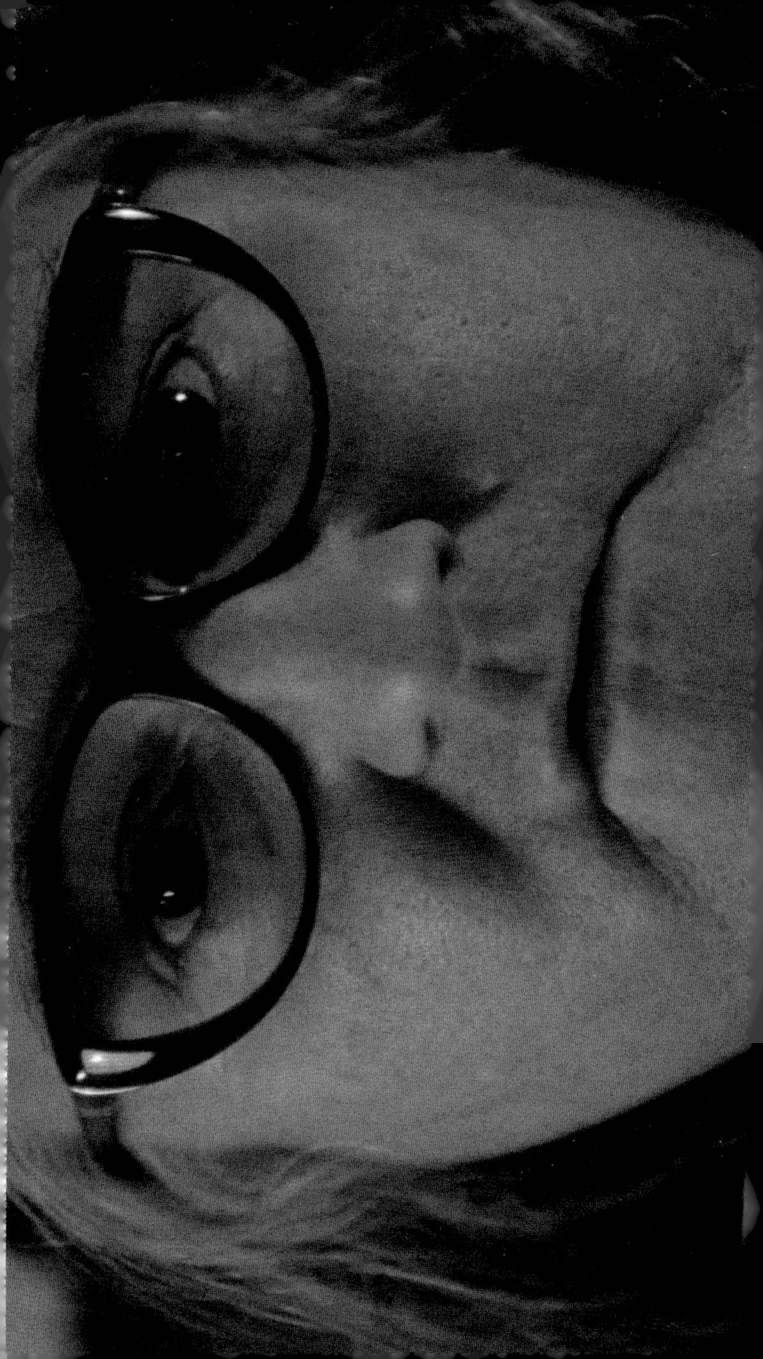

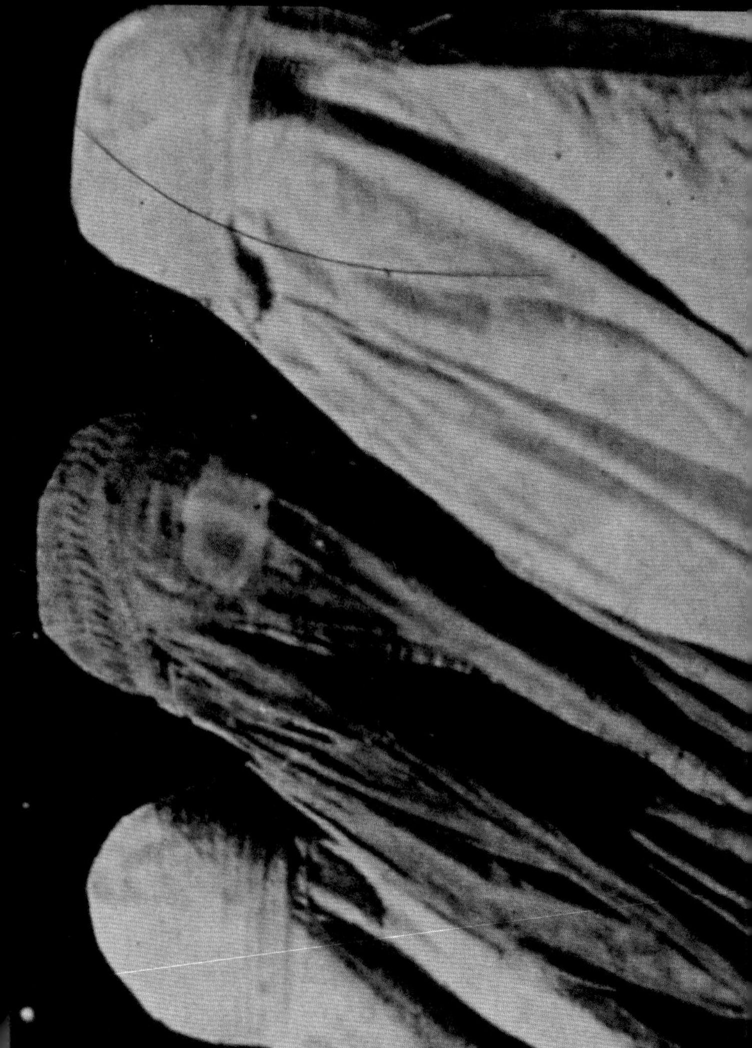

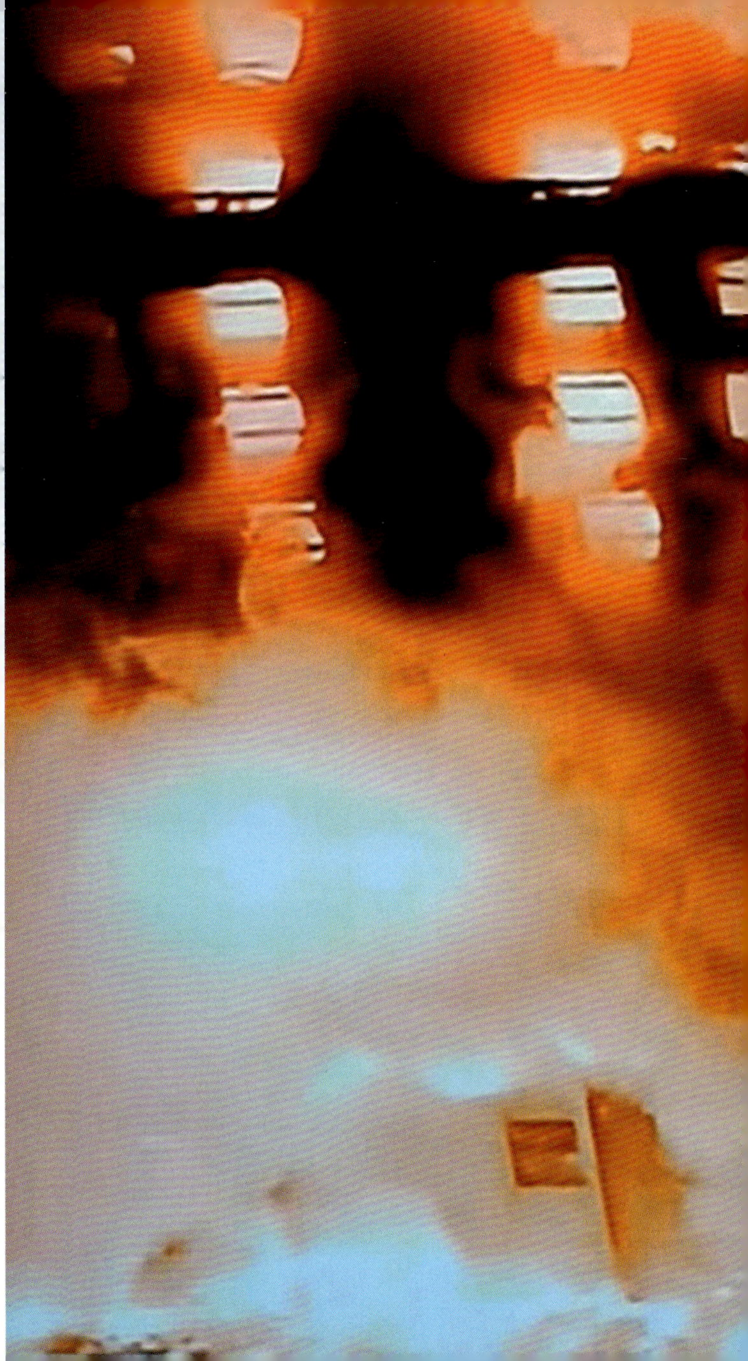

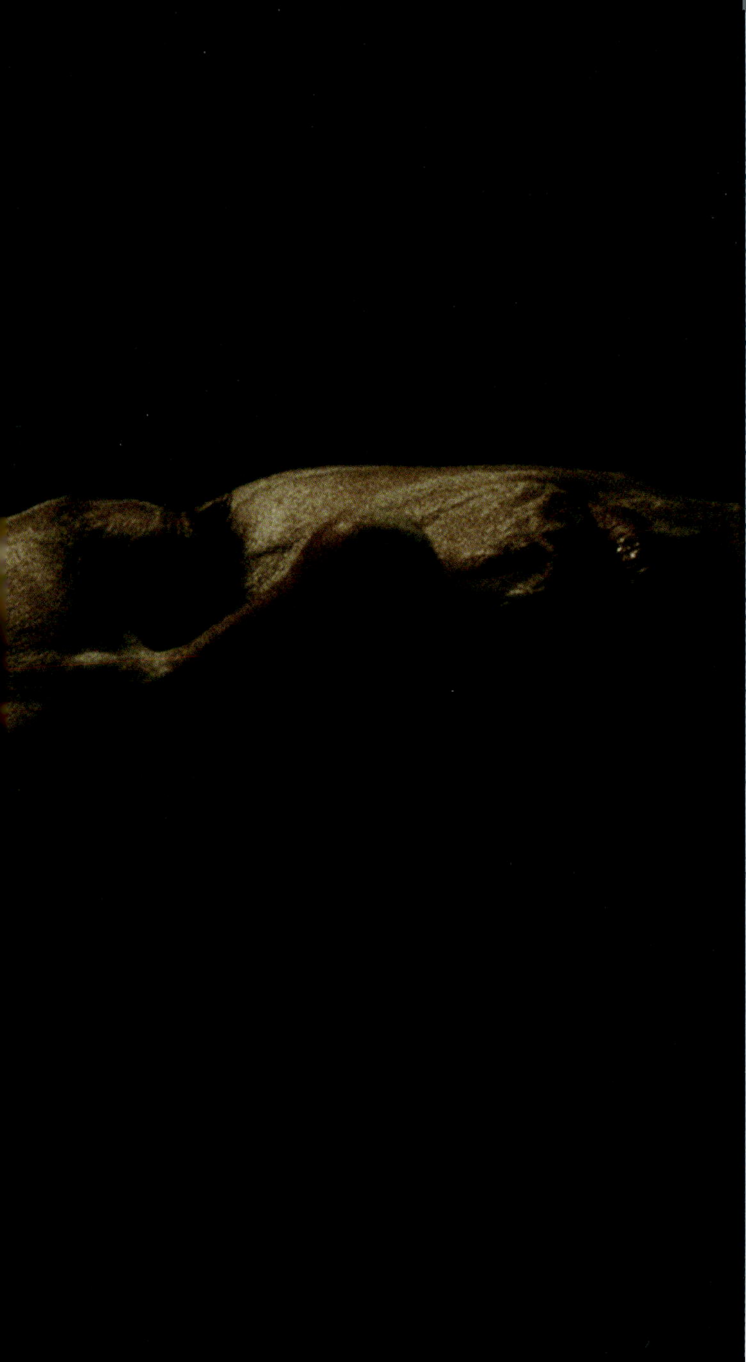

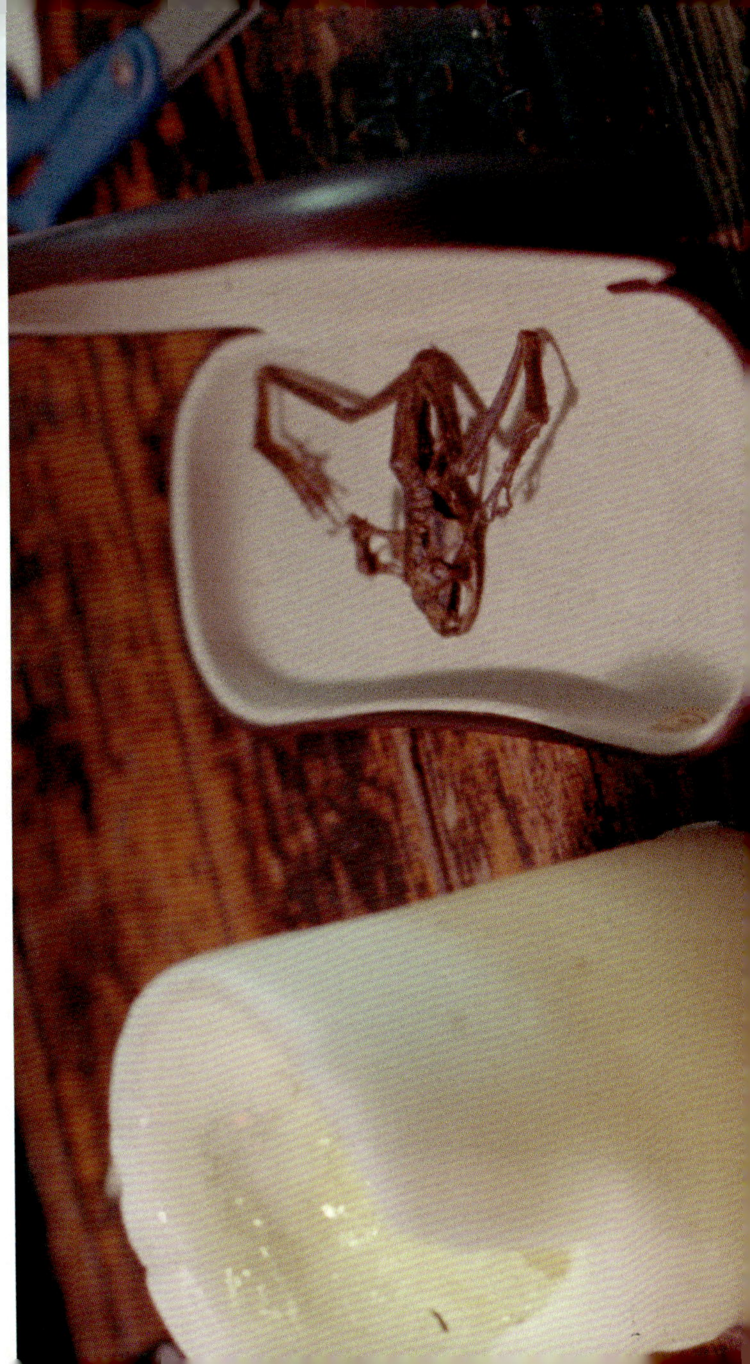

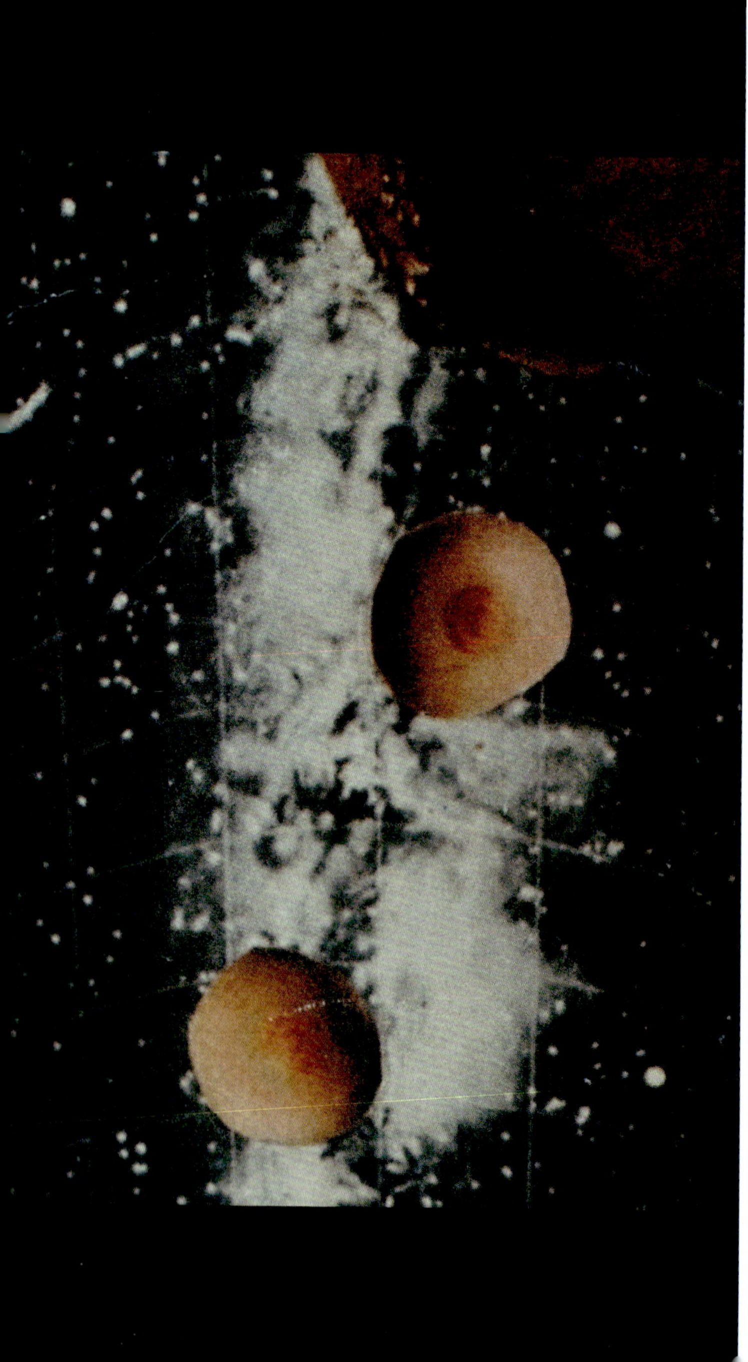

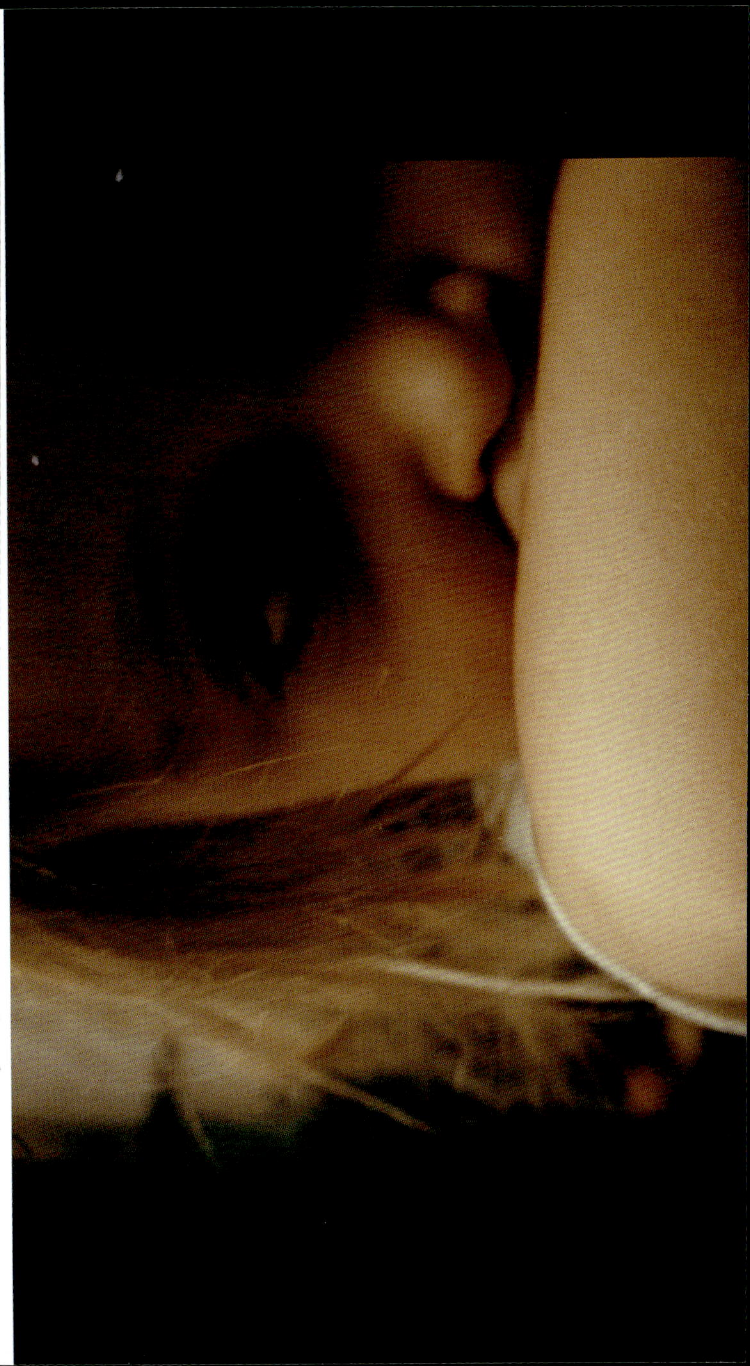

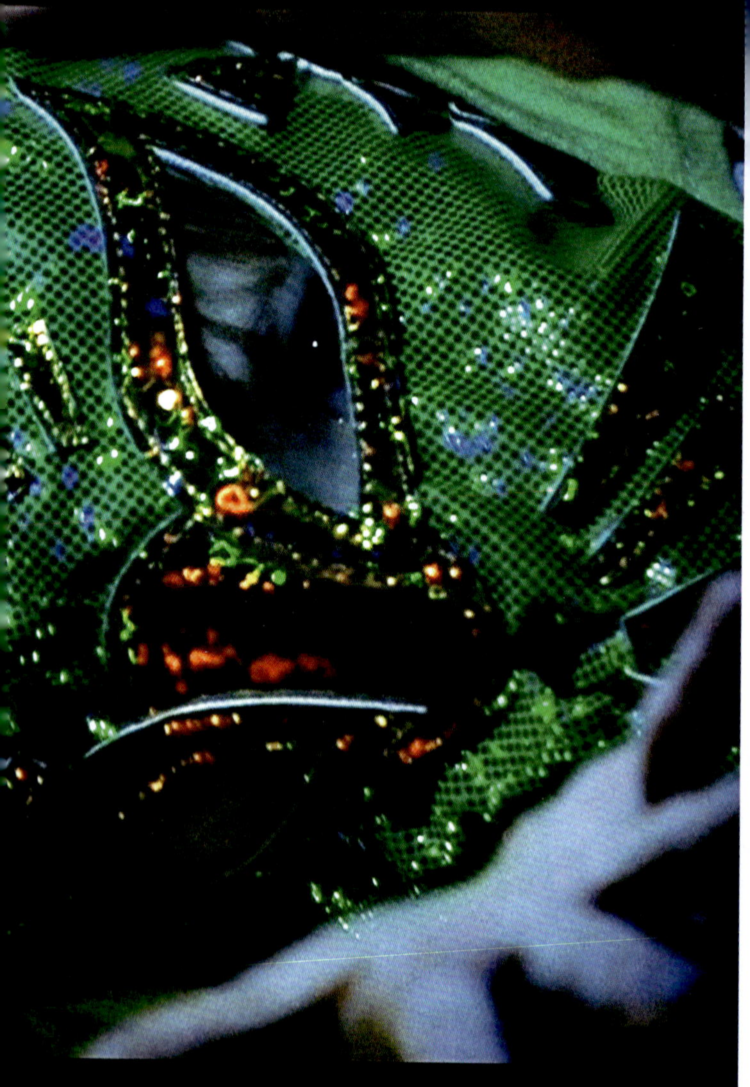

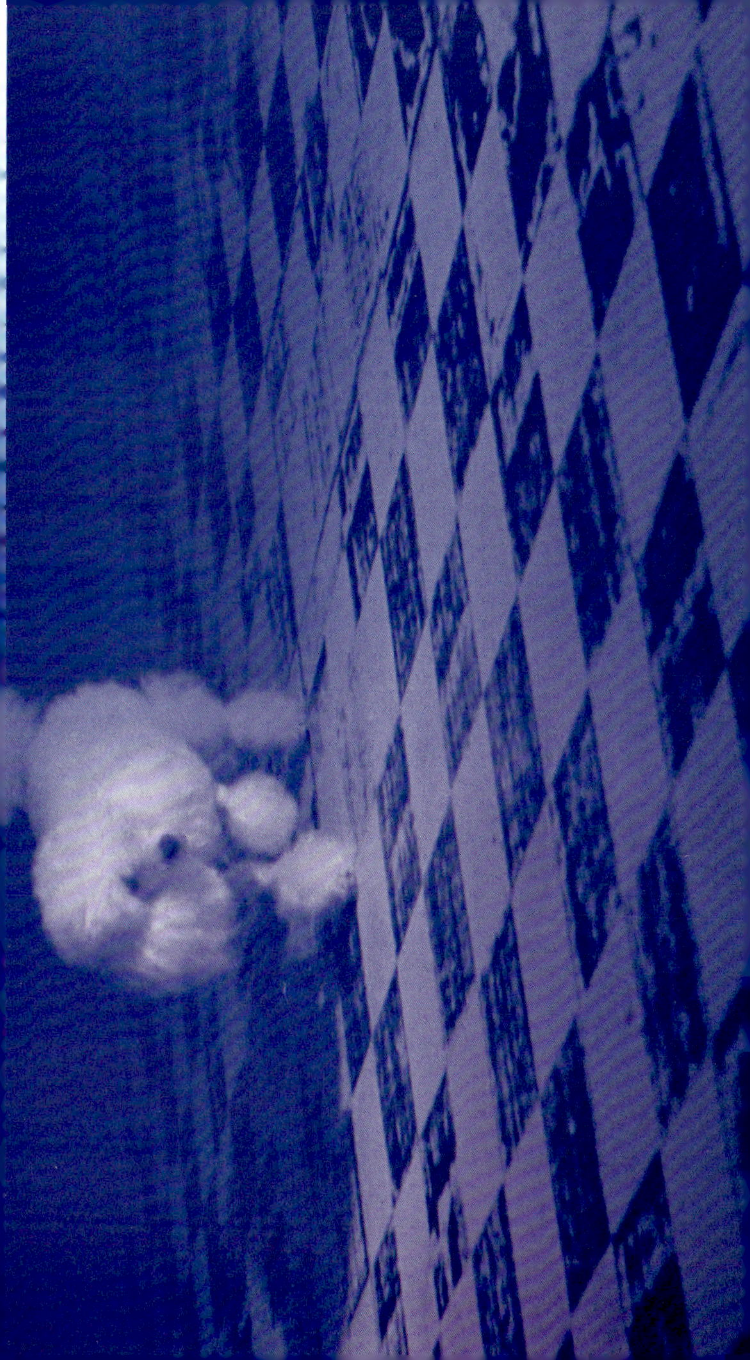

DEUX SOEURS QUI NE SONT PAS SOEURS (2019)

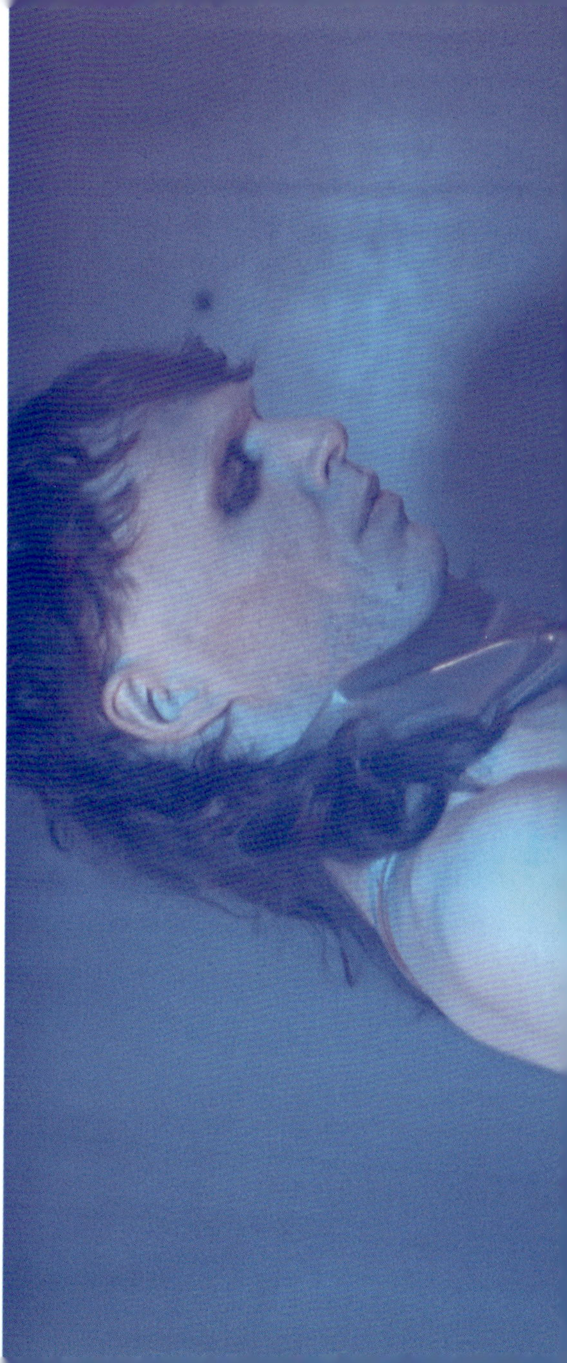

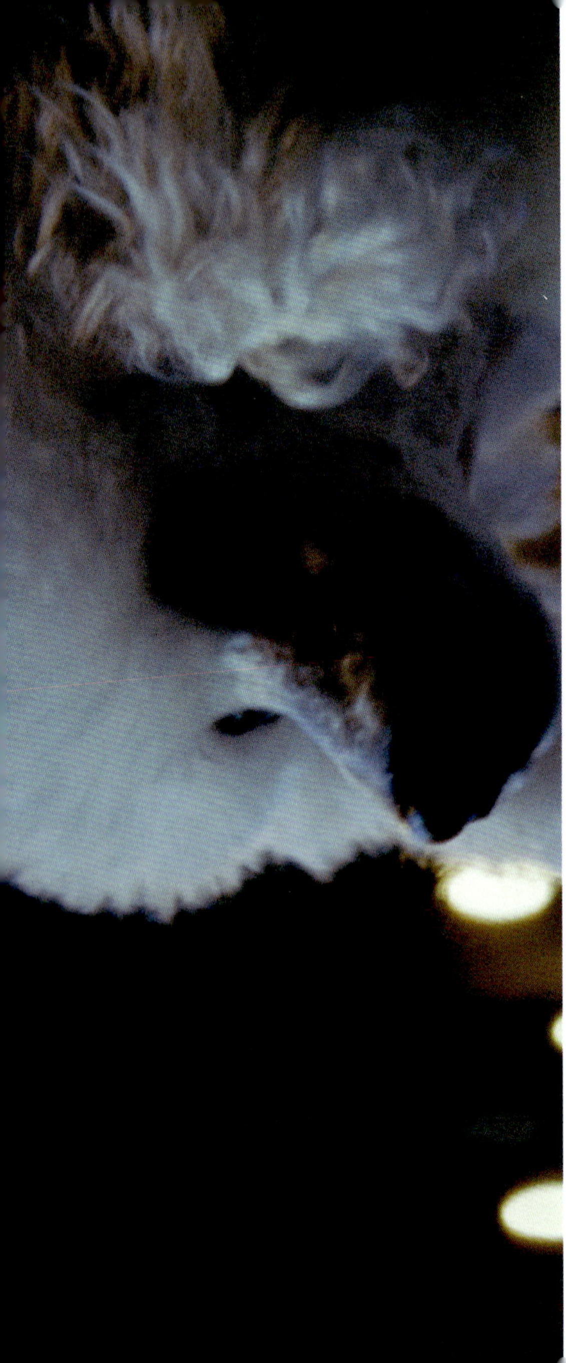

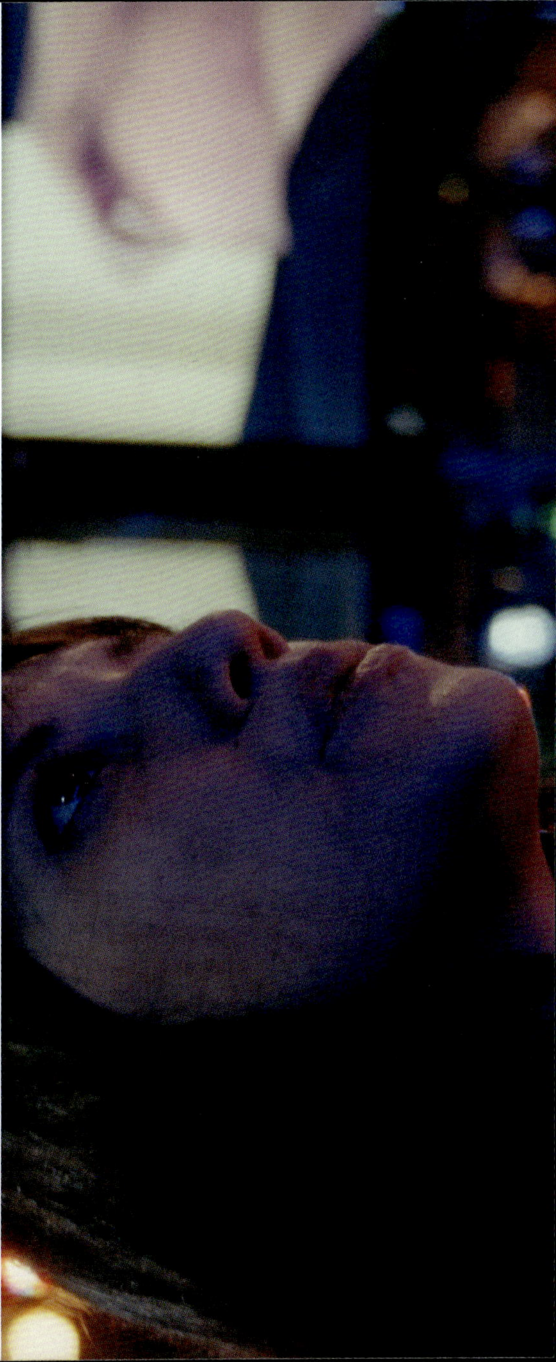

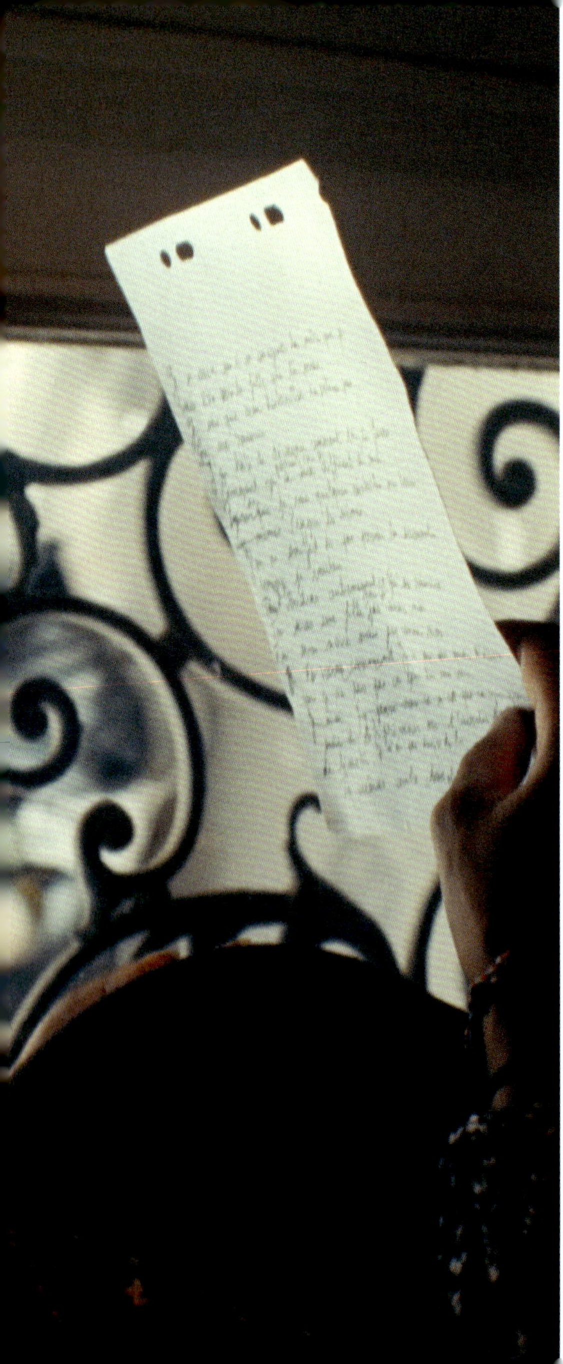

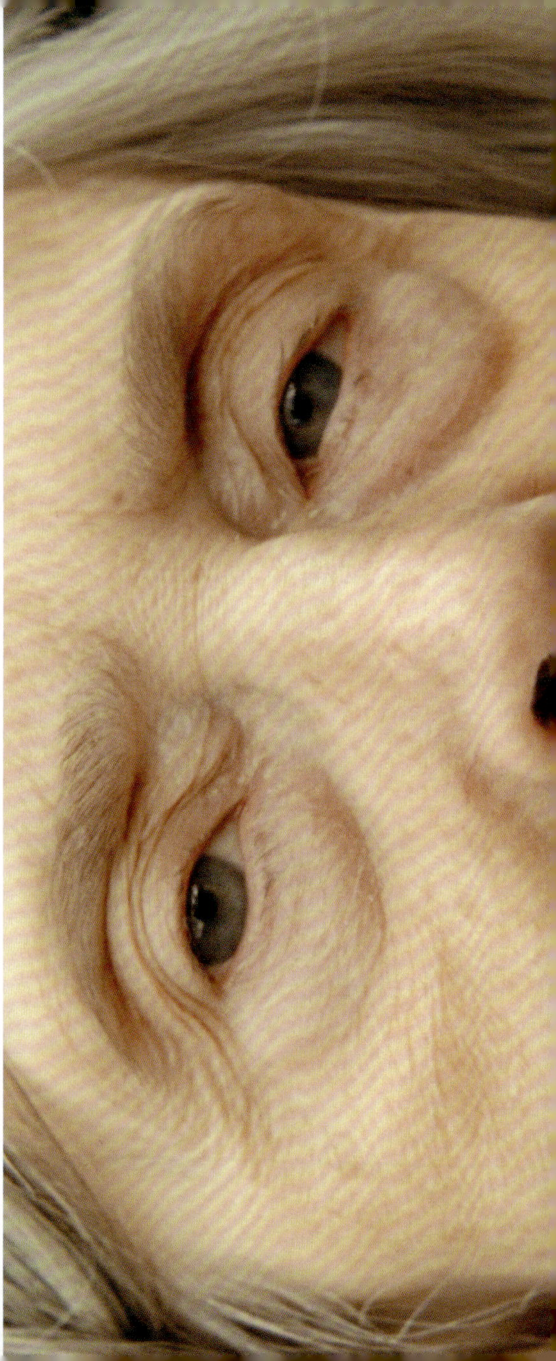

READER

SONIC MEDITATIONS
Pauline Oliveros

Introduction I

Sonic Meditations are intended for group work over a long period of time with regular meetings. No special skills are necessary. Any persons who are willing to commit themselves can participate. The ♀ Ensemble to whom these meditations are dedicated has found that non-verbal meetings intensify the results of these meditations and help provide an atmosphere which is conducive to such activity. With continuous work some of the following becomes possible with Sonic Meditations: Heightened states of awareness or expanded consciousness, changes in physiology and psychology from known and unknown tensions to relaxations which gradually become permanent. These changes may represent a tuning of mind and body. The group may develop positive energy which can influence others who are less experienced. Members of the Group may achieve greater awareness and sensitivity to each other. Music is a welcome by-product of this activity.

Introduction II

Pauline Oliveros has abandoned composition/performance practice as it is usually established today for Sonic Explorations which include everyone who wants to participate. She attempts to erase the subject/object or performer/audience relationship by returning to ancient forms which preclude spectators. She is interested in communication among all forms of life, through Sonic Energy. She is especially interested in the healing power of Sonic Energy and its transmission within groups.

All societies admit the power of music or sound. Attempts to control what is heard in the community are universal. For instance, music in the church has always been limited to particular forms and styles in accordance with the decrees of the Church Fathers. Music in the courts has been controlled through the tastes of patrons. Today, Muzak is used to increase or stimulate consumption in merchandising establishments.

Sonic Meditations are an attempt to return the control of sound to the individual alone, and within groups especially for humanitarian purposes; specifically healing.

Each Sonic Meditation is a special procedure for the following:

1. Actually making sounds
2. Actively imagining sounds
3. Listening to present sounds
4. Remembering sounds

Because of the special procedures involved, most all of the meditations are available to anyone who wishes to participate regardless, or in spite, of musical training. All that is required is a <u>willing commitment to the given conditions.</u>

Sound making during the meditations is primarily vocal, sometimes hand clapping or other body sounds, sometimes using sound producing objects and instruments.

Sound imagining is encouraged through the use of various questions designed to trigger auditory fantasy. Individuals are then asked to share what was heard inwardly, with members of the group using any means to describe the experience. Conditions given for listening to present sounds are intended to expand awareness of the auditory environment, both within and without of the individual.

Auditory memory is also encouraged by trigger questions with subsequent sharing of these memories in the group. Some of the meditations involve body movement as well. The term meditation is used simply to mean dwelling with or upon an idea, an object, or lack of object without distraction, or divided attention.

Healing can occur in relation to the above activities when 1) individuals feel the common bond with others through a shared experience, 2) when one's inner experience is made manifest and accepted by others, 3) when one is aware of and in tune with one's surroundings, and 4) when one's memories, or values, are integrated with the present and understood by others.

In process a kind of music occurs naturally. Its beauty is not through intention, but is intrinsically the effectiveness of its healing power. This may be felt by the group, and the music relates to the people who make it through participation and sharing, as a stream or river whose waters offer refreshment and cleansing to those who find it.

-I-

Teach Yourself to Fly

Any number of persons sit in a circle facing the center. Illuminate the space with dim blue light. Begin by simply observing your own breathing. Always be an observer. Gradually allow your breathing to become audible. Then gradually introduce your voice. Allow your vocal cords to vibrate in any mode which occurs naturally. Allow the intensity to increase very slowly. Continue as long as possible naturally, and until all others are quiet, always observing your own breath cycle.

Variation: Translate voice to an instrument.

-X-

Sit in a circle with your eyes closed. Begin by observing your own breathing. Gradually form a mental image of one person who is sitting in the circle. Sing a long tone to that person. Then sing the pitch that person is singing. Change your mental image to another person and repeat until you have contacted every person in the circle one or more times.

DOCTOR WILLIAMS' HEIRESSES
Alice Notley

Poe was the first one, he mated with a goddess. His children were Emily Dickinson & Walt Whitman—out of wedlock with a goddess. Then Dickinson & Whitman mated—since they were half divine they could do anything they wanted to—& they had two sons, William Carlos Williams & Ezra Pound, & a third son T. S. Eliot who went to a faraway country & never came back. From out of the West came Gertrude Stein, the daughter of the guy who wrote the 800-page novel & the girl who thought maybe rightly that she was Shakespeare. Gertrude Stein & William Carlos Williams got married: their two legitimate children, Frank O'Hara & Philip Whalen, often dressed & acted like their uncle Ezra Pound. However, earlier, before his marriage to Gertrude Stein, Williams had a child by the goddess Brooding. His affair with Brooding was long & passionate, & his child by her was oversized, Charles Olson. Before Charles Olson's birth the goddess had also been having an affair with Williams' brother Ezra Pound. No one was ever absolutely sure who the father of Olson was. Now O'Hara & Whalen were males that were male-female, as were many of the children of Williams by various goddesses & of Gertrude Stein & some gods. Olson was too big to be as male-female as he would have liked; his female was always curling up inside his shoulder or wrist to take a nice dark nap. Anyway it was striking how there were no females in this generation; & the first children of the male-females & of Olson & their other brothers were all males, and there were very many of them because of their fathers' incredible promiscuity. But the male-females also produced a second wave of children of which there were many females. These females could not understand how they came to be born—they saw no one among their parents & brothers who resembled them physically, for the goddesses their fathers mated with were evaporative non-parental types. As a matter of fact these females couldn't even believe that their fathers were their fathers. They came to indulge in a kind of ancestor worship—that is they each fell in love with a not too distant ancestor. One of them, Bernadette Mayer, fell in love with Gertrude Stein. And the one named Alice Notley fell in love with her grandfather, William Carlos Williams.

YOUTH AND BEAUTY

I bought a dishmop—
having no daughter—
for they had twisted
fine ribbons of shining copper
about white twine
and made a tousled head
of it, fastened it
upon a turned ash stick
slender at the neck
straight, tall—
when tied upright
on the brass wallbracket
to be a light for me
and naked
as a girl should seem
to her father.

* * *

— I can't remember anything about what I was thinking about Williams & women writers two years ago. It was just a crackbrained theory so I could write some works then.

— Why are you working up to writing some incredibly baroque lecture? You should be worrying about whether or not your panties are gonna fall down while you're giving it.

— Which pair should I wear in case they do?

— Your Philip Whalen black & white calligraphy panties with lower case letters stitched along the seams … Why don't you do something easy like play some records of Williams reading?

— Ah, they've all heard those records.

— Are you kidding? Young poets haven't heard shit—they all turn up their noses at the Caedmon records because they got famous on the Dylan Thomas records. Which is why we liked them.

— Helena has the Williams record.

— She wouldn't have it if it weren't for me. I embarrassed her to death by making her read in class that poem about the girdle. English guys are great. They don't care what any poem looks like
or where the lines break, they just start reading it like it was some more Tennyson & find themselves saying "I gotta/ buy me a new/ girdle." & "I GOTTA/ wig/gle/ for this."

— I remember these funny conversations you & I'd have in England, where I'd get all indignant about the way I imagined that Williams treated Flossie. Then you'd get very intense & say something about how when he was old he had to come crawling to her on his hands & knees in "Asphodel, That Greeny Flower."

— That business still makes me uncomfortable.

— Our conversations?

— No, Williams & Flossie. Even when they got married she owed him a debt …

— She did?

— I mean she owed him one, & then she kept on waiting & holding back about getting back at him. Meanwhile he would go out & be a bad boy some more.

— Do you remember anything about my theory regarding Williams offhand?

— What Williams did for you—he consolidated a lot of what you knew already, but he allowed you to be fast, perky, sassy, talky, all these different ways that had to do with talking, in one poem. He helped you to be as fast as you are. And to consolidate these voices you were hearing in your head & in the house & on the street & put them in the same poem. Getting it off Williams was like getting it authentic & not a little thirties-movies-modern like in Frank O'Hara … What I got off of him was a sharp clear use of direct address. He had this way of using the imperative tone.

— My theory had something to do with being for awhile the female to his male. You could use him without sounding like another imitation Williams poem. And how could you not use him since he was the greatest one? But you could use him to sound entirely new if you were a woman. It was all about this woman business. I thought we didn't need to read women—I mean find the hidden in the woodwork ones—so much as find the poems among whatever sex that made you feel free to say whatever you liked. Williams makes you feel that you can say anything, including your own anything.

— Well he made you feel like you could talk about your tampax without feeling tragic about it or even daring, just getting the exact register of annoyance or non-annoyance or whatever.

— He also made it so I could write about the kids, or not always about, but just include the kids. It's because of Williams that you can include everything that's things—& maybe everything that's words, is that going too far?—if you are only up to noticing everything that your life does include. Which is hard. Too many people have always already been telling you for years what your life includes ... Ha ha! I just remembered last week you said he was the rich man's Gertrude Stein. You're terrible!

— At least I don't have the hubris to address Williams directly in a poem. Like you. Holy Jesus!

— Well I was pregnant at the time, & he delivered babies. I had a crush on my obstetrician then too, remember him?

— That sonofabitch? He was the great guy who wrote me all those prescriptions for sleeping pills.

THE DISPUTANTS

Upon the table in their bowl!
in violent disarray
of yellow sprays, green spikes
of leaves, red pointed petals
and curled heads of blue

and white among the litter
of the forks and crumbs and plates
the flowers remain composed.
Coolly their colloquy continues
above the coffee and loud talk
grown frail as vaudeville.

* * *

"It seems really the body itself speaking, a very old,
very certain … and absolutely unflustered body …
It is the body speaking." "Begin then sisters of the
sacred well." "A 'fine' man or woman, let us say, goes
down. If this be not a necessary terminal act is it not
then in itself a work of art; an evocation of the true
procreative process which is at the back of all genius
& all worth?" And you like my poetry for my body,
& I admire it in the mirror to write my poetry, though
it is aging, though it is aging & that is admirable.
As a poet I study my physiology, I don't discourse
on the evils of alcohol & drugs. I would give you in my
poetry all the delight that my body might give your
eyes & hands or that any lively body might there are
so many—as a poet I study my physiology. This is
Alice speaking now, it's not my consciousness
I study but my physiology. My blood & my breathing,
my vision, my walk, the chapping of my lips, the
greying of my hair, my flowers becoming less sticky
more silky, the birds in my nests, etc. dirty jokes, a
tiny car drives down my neck and over my shoulder.
  Williams would have the man classify bodies:
"some a sort of hanging rind for the brain, some fit
only to bear offspring, some absolutely not, some
flowers, some this & some that, etc. And all requiring
refertilization, both male & female, one way or another
at frequent intervals." But he would be at least in
a poem any body he so classified—the bug under
a waterfall of piss.

One time I had a dream that I was a flea & then in the dream I grew up to become the ballerina Maria Tallchief. Is that Williams—the first Native American ballerina? Someone, Edwin, didn't like her as much as Frank did. This is the body speaking—the physiology of my vision is also clouds & sky & grass & paintings. My skin makes words—fingertip & tongue. Let's touch tongues.

Sometimes I'm just looking at the shows but sometimes I get so angry, & what I think I'm angry about is phantasmic & this anger will drag me down—a "fine" woman, another flea, a secret prima ballerina—how similar are anger & lust? I can't stand it, I can't stand it. I exult in it, I triumph.

SAPPHO, BE COMFORTED

There is only one love
let it be a sparrow
to hold between the breasts
greets us daily with its small cries

what does it matter?
I, we'll say, love a woman
but truth to tell
I love myself more. Sappho loves

the music of her own
songs which men seldom
mean to her, a lovely girl
of whom she is desperately fond:

This is myself though
my hateful mirror
shows every day my big nose.
Men are indifferent to me, my sweet
but I would not trade

my skill in composition for
all, a second choice, you
present for my passionate caresses.

* * *

... theory which I still have but temporarily can't locate, & we've had no heat or hot water now for five days plus is anyone interested? "It's like, there's still no decent book by a critic on him—no essay that isn't patronizing or evasive & the way poets know about him they don't say much, it's too personal knowing about Williams. Meanwhile the critics (this is Ted speaking) have given us first the Eliot Era then the Pound Era, while Williams is over there being the real whole thing." "Where is Hugh Kenner from?" I said. "That's a good question," he said, " ... from Harvard." "He's picked out this one thing Williams does," I said, "of delaying or omitting verbs & talks about it as this great discovery-trick of Williams,' without noticing that's also how we talk around here in America. That poem "Young Sycamore" is in the syntax of conversation." "Hugh Kenner thinks poets are as smart as he is," he said. "I don't feel like paideumaing again," I said. "I like Hugh Kenner," he said, "I like critics who are brilliant but long & dull." "I like anybody else but critics to be like that," I said. "I consider that to be a perfect exchange between us," he said. "There's nothing I like critics to be like yet," I said.

Let's get bitchy about a few things, he in effect said. What about this "the local," isn't that a little overrated? what about all those things he's supposed to be that he isn't? Oh, I said, local was a word he used to explain why Poe wrote horror stories that took place in horror-story land. Long stupid exchange about the local. Like, The most local thing about a person is their body I said, for some it's their brain he said, etc. What about Lowell? he said, does everyone think Williams was just being stupid about Robert Lowell? Ask your audience in multiple choice form: a) although Williams was a great poet he was stupid b) he made a mistake that day c) ... I blanked out for a while & came back when he was saying, if women get mad at Williams they can't dismiss him, they're engaged with him & call him "You man, you!" Now you (meaning me) you got to read Williams from the very first face to face, that way where you're not involved with technique. That's unusual for a poet, but he really reached you. You read him for yourself. Yes, I said, I don't want to deal with the poems right now because I don't want to ruin them for me, even for a little while, by holding them up & taking them apart in public.

The rest of our conversation was about the variable foot, & that conversation mostly evaporated, so I'll invent something, this:

> We still haven't caught up with what
> Williams meant by the variable foot, which
> has to do with scoring for tone of voice,
> which is part of your music & your breath,
> but maybe even more. Variable foot is
> maybe about the dominance of tone of
> voice over other considerations—I do my
> poems this way 'cause I talk from here—
> haven't you ever talked to anyone? I'm
> not an oracle or a musical instrument or
> a tradition or a stethoscope or a bellows
> or even a typewriter: I am a tone of voice,
> warming, shifting, pausing, changing,
> including, asserting, exulting, including,
> including, turning & including. I break my
> lines where I do, as I'm being as various
> as my voice should be in our intimacy. I'd
> like there to be something as firm as you
> to push my voice into its best most natural
> place, that would really be measure.
> But I like to lay them out in dropped-line

triplets, three's are good for me, because
I can go on at length say addressing you
in that way where you'll hear me out—
Flossie it's me with our fifty years together
included in how I intone each word so
you must hear me out. If you do the world
does, though I'll never hear about it.

I do not come to you
save that I confess
to being
half man and half
woman. I have seen the ivy
cling
to a piece of crumbled
wall so that
you cannot tell
by which either
stands: this is to say
if she to whom I cling
is loosened both
of us go down.

* * *

in lifting your skirts to show your silken
crotches, it is this that is intended.
You are it.

I was your nightgown,
I watched!

FROM AN INTERVIEW:

"I think about him more than anybody. I mean he's
the greatest poet of the century, there's no way

around that & I think you have to go back to Williams when you start."

"The thing about William Carlos Williams is, aside from the fact that he talked & wrote in this very particular way, he sets himself up to be this character of the American male in this way. And besides being the most important American poet. So if you're a woman you can relate to him in this way, where you'll be the woman, the typical American woman character. He made himself be this character, so you can make yourself be this other character, the polar opposite of him, & it enables you to have access to his secrets & to his diction & to his ways of thinking … I don't know there's this way to be yourself, a woman, & person that has a lot to do with William Carlos Williams … There's Williams. In this century, there's Williams. It's actually a secret you know, in spite of everything—it's still a secret … it's still our secret."

"Well, if you're a woman you put yourself somewhere near the beginning & then there's this other place where you put yourself in terms of everybody."

"These are childish activities. To go look at the flowers, I mean in a way, to go to a place that is a house for flowers & look at the flowers … To go & see this movie for a child & then to go to, into the part of the aquarium where all the children hang around & stare over the railing at all the crocodiles & alligators, which never move … They just sit there. Do you think I have a childish voice? I probably do."

"In that poem."
"I don't mind having one. I don't mind being accused of having one. I don't feel a necessity for being a mature person in this world, I don't think too many poets really are, but men are very good at acting out

the part. They've been brought up to have a good cover story, but they're all kids too—the male poets."

"I mean all the grownups in this world, they're just playing house. All the poets know they're playing house."

"Yeah, but I'm a character too. I'm the character of the new wife, & the new mother. It's a speech actually, a sort of a dramatic speech … And this character is making a speech on a stage like a character in Shakespeare, & the stage is sort of dark except for the light around the person talking … this poem I became the voice of the woman who's a wife & a mother. It was also me the poet."

"I think it's very interesting that things close down & open up at the same time … Life is always closing down on you as you get older & older, all you can hope to do is open it up."

"I would hope that the poems would be like that actually. A woman just came in & was there & said a few things & then left & you had this sense that she was actually there. And maybe she was me, & maybe she wasn't. Just some woman."

"Awkward, spasmodic—my sense of rhythm. I don't know, I've gone through periods where I didn't want to think about rhythm at all, it seemed so incredibly arbitrary. And so I would use the most arbitrary rhythms there were … So since I've been writing a lot by hand in the last few years, I would just break—if I had a notebook the size of this book, & I was writing in script & broke the line at the end of the page, when I typed it up it would turn out to look like a regular kind of line length for a poem, & I would break my lines that way, it gave me a kind of fierce pleasure to do that … And then this new music has come on … But I don't know what the system is exactly. It varies from line to line & from poem to poem."

"I used to think that all my poems had the rhythms of 1950s popular songs, you know, pre-rock & roll songs, it always seemed to me that my poems should be sung by Georgia Carr, or somebody like that …"

"I'm not very familiar with *How To Write*."

" … I love flowers, I identify with them. I think that they are these beings. I'm always conscious of flowers being these beings … they're these other people from this other world … Well it's all this sense that this flower is this very fragile thing, but it's also very strong, & you know that poem "The rose unbruised penetrates space" & if you look at a flower very closely that's what the petals do. Flowers are a very fragile thing, but it's a totally penetrating thing. And it has this edge & the edge is very cutting & the edge is very fragile at the same time & it has this total strength out of being so strongly colored & out of being so perfect too."

"Being a woman the poet? Well it's a tone of voice that people aren't used to. You have to hit these tones of voice that people are going to say are this or that, strident or shrill …"

"I don't really want to be a character that way, it's just something you do when you make a poem … I'm not all that interested in being a woman, it's just a practical problem that you deal with when you write poems. You do have to deal with the problem of who you are so that you can be a person talking."

THE LOVE CHARM

Take this, the nexus
of unreality,
my head, I detach
it for you. Take it

in your hands, metal
to eat out
the heart, if held
to the heart. Hold it

to your heart
and wait, only wait
the while
its fissions curdle.

* * *

Jan 17, 1980

Dear Alice,

If Dr. Williams married Gertrude Stein, is that why my typewriter will occasionally refuse to make spaces between the words as if I were a Greek or Latin poet? It would be nice if Gertrude Stein had actually given birth to children, so she could have written all about it and then if they were delivered by her husband Dr. Williams, preferably at home, he could have written all about it too, just like Sigmund Freud's midwife, his mother's midwife, who predicted he'd be famous because he'd howled peculiarly or maybe it was something about the moon, you'd better look that up. And if of course Gertrude Stein had given birth to one of our mothers who then gave birth to us, or one of our fathers, Mr. or Mrs. Stein-Carlos-Williams or Mrs. Stein-Carlos-Williams-what?, who would my mother have married if she were Gertrude Stein's daughter, Mrs. Stein-Carlos, Williams-Hemingway maybe, what would I be, like Margaux or Mariel now today? Maybe my father would've been Donald Sutherland or even Larry Rivers! But in either case I might be a lunatic or a socialite, though I know this kind of speculation is not your intention. Now this baby inside me is doing everything short of howling, pushing me around incredibly, I have a cold and the midwife says you won't go into labor if you have a cold, so now I've a bad one for two weeks but there was something else I wanted to say. Did I tell you my students, when I talked about Dr. Williams and made them read him, all for the first time, found him to be reactionary, they thought he was ordinary, they thought his poetry was just like what old-fashioned poetry was like to them. And there is a situation in this house that relates to this. We rent this house from a child psychiatrist who gets insulted if he's called a psychologist because that means somebody hasn't noticed he's an M.D. Now I don't know if this is all worth going into, but it's a way of avoiding saying anything literary—there's this other person, a painter named Arthur Yanoff who's a friend of both Paul Metcalf's and Russell Banks', who is a close friend of the doctor's, in our case, Dr. K, and this Arthur was the one who led us to this house and he is so impressed with doctors and with a doctor's credentials and identity as to render himself practically the child in the face of it and Dr. K seems pleased by this kind of vulnerability, in fact when we listen to Dr. K fighting with his girlfriend, it's obvious he takes advantage of his doctorhood and plays the role of the allknowing fatherhood to make her feel unsure of herself & thus the pawn. I myself have always been impressed with doctors, not doctors like this Dr. K, who seems to know nothing, but ones like Dr. Williams who seem to encompass everything as if a doctor-poet, a general practitioner as it were, was the only representative of what might be called the contemporary American hermetic tradition, not that I'd believe a word they said … So now I have to talk about Doctor Williams, and I remember what I started out to say before, it's another excuse not to talk about him quite yet—when I was ordering books for my classes and one of them was his *Imaginations* the woman at the bookstore had me spell out his full name and then she said, gee it's amazing what mothers will name their children nowadays. Let's see, I always see Williams in the tradition of Dante so that *Spring and All* becomes his *Vita Nuova* or maybe *Kora in Hell* does and then *Paterson* becomes *The Divine Comedy*. Then again there is the question of "The Red Wheelbarrow" or does it even have a title? so much depends upon, and so on … It was written on the blackboard when I was in high school and I can still see it and recite it much the same as I can do with Emily Dickinson's "I'm nobody who are you …" but somehow, as I've made these two poems be opposites, I associate the one, the wheelbarrow of course, with all my ideas and instigations and inspirations to write poetry and the other, the being nobody, wlth all the Catholic teachings on humility which might actually prevent that from happening. So that it always seemed to me from Williams I could deduct that the wonderful capacity for the world to exist without an I was good for me and that the rest of a person's studies of him or her self ought to be relegated to prose which I later noticed he had sort of done too. Although I know in saying that I'm not being entirely accurate, but I am just telling you my adolescent fantasies about what could or couldn't get done in writing well. Then again all this also made me think that women were more Catholic than men and for a long time I took Williams' hard-nosed attitude about things (by this I don't mean things) to be the result of his being a man although I knew the same womanly sensation could result from, say, my reading Catullus or even everyone, if I could only get beyond my own self-conscious judgments about poetry. That's why I always liked the French writers. So this is my memoir of Wm. Carlos Williams! I've always been very grateful to him for resuscitating the prose mixed with poetry form which is a form I like and seems like a good form to be in a hurry in. I like what he says about Yorkville and about having babies, oh god I hope I never have to be a literary critic to earn my livelihood, I'd rather be a doctor any day, the doctor who delivered me was named Peter Neyland. He was rather a bad doctor but he had fantastic offices full of giant palms and leather chairs and vials of stuff. You see you started all this by keeping on referring to Williams as the doc. I've often wondered why all the pretentious people who talk all the time about "Olson" don't refer to him rather as "Charles" or the something. For many years, for all the years I had a car, I would always carry around the complete poems of Wm. Carlos Williams in my trunk because I always thought it was somehow necessary to have them there, just like I read somewhere about a taxi-driver, or actually it was that I met one once who told me that he always had a case of beer in his trunk because he knew that no matter what the exigencies of driving around NY might turn out to be, that would be all that he needed. Then sadly when I no longer had a car I found the condition of my Williams books to be awful and when Lewis and I put our books together, he excoriated me on my lack of devotion to the books but it was really just the opposite of that! Well if any more maybe more abstruse or profound thoughts do come, you can be sure I'll be sending them or unless the baby comes first—you ever have a baby when you had a cold?

Love,
Bernadette

LINES

Leaves are grey green,
the glass broken, bright green.

* * *

"The first line in the first poem reads 'Innosense can never perish.' I really believed that then, & I really believe it now. It is something intrinsic in a man."

"I won't have to powder my nose tonight 'cause
Billie's gonna take me home in his car—
The perfect type of the man of action is the suicide."

"What then of a life such as mine? I say that Chaucer, Villon & Whitman were contemporaries of mine with whom I am constantly in touch—through the art of writing. They are worthy rivals ..."

"I was very late, very slow to find out about the world ... The real thing is I didn't know *anything* about life. I was completely ignorant."

"I endowed her with magic qualities. She had seized me from my mother as her special possession, adopted me, & her purpose in life was to make me her own. But my mother ended all that with a terrific clap in the puss."

"Somehow poetry & the female sex were allied in my mind. The beauty of girls seemed the same to me as the beauty of a poem. I knew nothing at all about the sexual approach but I had to do something about it. I did it in the only terms I knew. Through poetry."

"The rhythmic pace was the pace of speech, an excited pace because I was excited when I wrote.

I was discovering, pressed by some violent mood."

"When I spoke of flowers, I *was* a flower, with all the prerogatives of flowers, especially the right to come alive in the spring."

"I was looking for a metric figure—a new measure. I couldn't find it & I couldn't wait for it. I was too impatient; I had to write."

"Something of this sort is what Oscar Wilde must have meant when he said, God created man, then woman, then the child & finally the doll. And the greatest of these was the doll."

"I thought of myself as springtime & I felt I was on my way to Hell (but I didn't go very far)."

"I've always thought of a poet as *not* a successful man except in his own mind, which is devoted to something entirely different than what the world thinks of as success."

"The whole book was written in an excited frame of mind. Floss helped with the research; I was working against time. She is solely responsible for Aaron Burr; she told me what she read, told it so graphically & vividly I sat down & wrote the whole thing in one sitting. She was satisfied & I was relieved, but I should confess right here that I never read a single book on him!"

"'I've never understood what upset you about it,' Mrs. Williams said. But the Doctor refused to retract; something about the very phrase anti-poetic apparently enraged him as a poet."

" … I'd always wanted to write a book about a baby.

I thought I knew what a baby was … I was filled up with babies & I wanted to write about them. The devil was in me … I was crazy about babies, the contempt that all babies have for adults. They don't give a damn what goes on & they let go with everything they have & sometimes it's not too attractive."

"I'll die before I've said my fill about women. I feel I am saying flattering things about them but they won't take it … I am so terribly conscious of woman as woman that it is hard for me to write about a woman—I become self-conscious—too aware that she is there ready to tell me I've got her all wrong."

"I knew the reader, any reader, would be interested in scandal so scandal went in …"

"At Wellesley once, they practically carried me off on their shoulders. I was speechless. You could hear a pin drop. A million girls were there … at least it looked that way. A bell kept ringing, it finally stopped. Floss had asked me to read the Coda to 'Asphodel' … I thought I didn't have time … but they stood on their heels & yelled … the girls … my God I was breathless, but I said do you really want more & they said yes so I read what Floss knew they would like. They were so adorable. I could have raped them all!"

"However, we're talking of the art of writing well in a modern world & women haven't much to do with that, I guess. Not directly. America is still too crude for that. I don't think any place is much better … Of course it's ridiculous to think of any land, as a land, in this respect. Women are as various (and as rare) as men."

"And who are you anyway?—with your small personal limitations of age, sex, & other sundry features like race & religion?

Unimportant.

You, even you are at the moment—the artist, good or bad—but a new creature.

You must let yourself go—release it …
… you are nature in action."

WINTER TREES

All the complicated details
of the attiring and
the disattiring are completed!
A liquid moon
moves gently among
the long branches.
Thus having prepared their buds
against a sure winter
the wise trees
stand sleeping in the cold.

* * *

He said say about flowers, say how when you write flowers, are flowers, it's like the way I perceive flowers. I wouldn't say perceive, it's the way I experience them—sometimes little to do with how I see them. I open your red & white book at random to "The Pot of Flowers." It's funny for you 'cause you don't tell which kind of flowers—what this one contains is flowers not particularly named flowers—the setting is strange to me too—you say what you see but the words you choose—it's a lamp & flowers isn't it? The effects of the flowers & light are so heady, that they aren't their names they're the headiness of flowers & light, pink flowers & white made mauve & red petals aslant darkened with mauve

red where in whorls
petal lays its glow upon petal
round flamegreen throats

It's a drunk-making poem till you include the leaves the flowerpot "and there, wholly dark, the pot/ gay with rough moss." That's very rich, but I've sobered just so it's in focus, the pot has edges & holds up the flowers. This is very funny this poem, instead of showing all medievally the respective virtues of the flower & the leaf—it's the flower & the flowerpot, & you do make us like the flowerpot as much as the flowers. This poem is from *Spring and All* so I check out the prose that goes with it in the original in *Imaginations*—you say some stuff about Dora Marsden & President Wilson & spring & hope—& I remember, I think, that this is a famous poem. Famous where? famous somewhere. But the guys who make the poems famous usually like the ones in quatrains or couplets. This one has that look, before you read it, like it might not hold up—my favorite kind of poem—& it looks like what it says. It looks like love that way. And I'm very tired tonight.

* * *

2 hours later

After a brief spasm of hysteria just now (2:45 AM), a thin ignoble thing taking the form of yelling at my husband because I couldn't finish didn't have the time writing this which is a talk anyway about you—as if it somehow had to be even better than whatever it might ever have been—I started to remember some things about the time when I addressed you directly (as in hubris, according to Ted) in my long poem

"Songs For The Unborn Second Baby." I believe
I even told you I hated you, though only I said "just
now." That poem has been recently published—am
I trying to make up for what I said? Well, no. Well,
maybe. But I remember, it was in England, & I was
very darkly depressed from having had a first child &
being pregnant with another, thought I was mad
murderous etc., & so isolated in this country town.
And how many pregnant women who were how I was
then you must have talked to—& how many couldn't
talk to each other about it—I couldn't find a female
confidante then, but I could talk to my husband,
especially, & my doctor (surprisingly), & Dante &
Philip Whalen & you. I wrote a letter to Philip & said
something like, I can't remember how I said it, some-
thing like, "What's the good of love anyway?" Or "Tell
me about love, is it of any use?" He wrote back & told
me good. Anyway, I wrote myself through this busi-

ness, this blackness which I'll no doubt go through
somehow again, in my poem. Before that though
I typed up, in its entirety, your poem "Asphodel, That
Greeny Flower," & Honey that took a long time. In
that bad time there was always you. To love as a
poet & to love & hate as a man. Immobile pregnant &
isolate & unhappy, I didn't need to read about your
attractions to women other than your wife. Your
reasoning seemed specious & was enraging … I'm
looking for a passage from "Asphodel" about a "field
of women like flowers & what should you do but love
them?" Everything that's catching my eye though,
in this poem, is something that's beautiful & makes
me cry. But to a pregnant woman, I repeat, your
reasoning was useless & enraging. We poets take
all words personally. But I wrote my poem & I used
for its form your *Paterson* & an O'Hara ode & those
Cantos … & it is held together by flowers, as
"Asphodel" is—we had a bewilderingly luxuriant
garden there—& by the presence of the opposite sex

"you" & by the will to write poetry. I want to say this only for me I think, I think whoever hears this knows it & knows all about you—I asked about love & Philip said yes, love, & your great poem is about how it itself is being that & being handed as that as a flower to your wife & how it "gelds the bomb"—no fear of evil death war destruction or pregnancy childbirth—because this poem exists. I suspected then & know now that that's true. And because you had written so, I was able to write & love & live, I don't even ever hate you temporarily anymore,

Yours,
Alice

Alice Notley
Jan 19–Feb 7, 1980

PAINTED CLEAR, PAINTED BLACK
Eileen Myles

I feel like the back story of Marjorie's avant garde mandate is mourning. I think Perloff has sustained an enormous amount of loss in her life and along with her championing of avant garde practice in her criticism she's also deeply engaged in controlling the emotional climate of the room she's in. Who gets to feel what when, and how! And that's a problem because poetry is a community not an institution and we're always at multiple purposes here in this room. When she opens her piece with Jed Rasula's assertion of the problem of there being too many poets I wonder why neither of them notice that in the mainstream there aren't any poets. We're mainly hearing that *no* poets are being read. That there's no understanding of poetry today. Then the writer, whoever cites something they used to like or understands *as* poetry. Anything will do because poetry has no *relevance*. The enterprise that all of us take part in is for all intents and purposes absent in public life today. Poetry is the absolutely denied body of free and democratic exchange. Poetry's where men get to feel like women always feel. Cause we're really just not there. I agree with Marjorie that what gets rewarded is mostly pretty damn boring. But that's because there is *no scene*. No excess. It just doesn't get any public ink. And this denial seems to be the empire moment. And it's why it doesn't matter to me how many poets there are. The most visible poets, the most rewarded poets are literally the ones who aren't. So in Perloff's response to Matvei's response to her original piece in *Boston Review* which was originally in *Virginia Quarterly Review* (and that's what she meant) she bothers to declare me to be a contemporary example of "transparency or feigned transparency" in poetry and I think if what she means is that my front story (unlike hers) is mourning she is absolutely right. In theory transparency used to mean that one could in some ways witness the process of the person writing. The writer was including the reader somehow. Later it referred to a kind of *aha* moment when the writer revealed an authentic self that showed all too well the workings of empire. Is that what she means that I do? In my empire of the heart. While feigning or not?

To reflect on my own writing I arrived on the scene in New York in my twenties (okay I already wrote a book about this) landing very deliberately in the avant garde where it seemed everyone I met took it upon himself to pass on to me "ze avant garde canon" as he saw it. There were so many approaches and rightnesses and because I already came from a doctrinaire catholic background I wasn't so open to learning from some man of my age or older "the truth." My avant garde then & now was composed of a shaky imagined grid holding a multiple of approaches. I did a magazine called *dodgems* that exemplified that. I published Charles and I published Alice Notley and I published Lily Tomlin. And I am always negotiating feeling and the day. Feeling lets me know when to duck and take space. How to edit. I think of the reader as somebody who deserves something other than a recitation from the long phallic night of my heart whether that recitation takes the form of personal expression or a wily conceptual sound poem. I like an author who is aware of reception and the body. If I think of transparency it's the text revealing the author, it's the text responding to the political environment, it's a distressed recording of the history of sexual violence on women, a map of mourning and a borrow from each thing I'm reading that has some impact on how writing stops and starts and what entirely it could do. There's also kind of an ethnic class-based regional bicycle I ride, which is a very familiar but always updating kind of speech pattern that feels to me like home. I know "we" hate speech but also we don't. Nobody hates speech. That's hyperbole. When I first read Gary Snyder I saw that his pacing was very particular and it reminded me in its way of the bodily traces in the speech balloons of comic books and I knew I could do something similar and I do. As a writer one is always thrifting. The works that Perloff ultimately loves are triumphs of that approach. Interestingly in the theory world outside of poetry *feeling* is hot stuff. Lots and lots of books. And it's true in the tier of poets that Matvei cites to Marjorie that she sneers at (academics are sort of like landlords. I'm not coming to *your* tiny apartment today. I'm working on *this*.) but in fact CAConrad, Ariana Reines, Daniel Borzutzky, Jenny Zhang, Dana Ward, Dottie Lasky, Simone White, and Karen Weiser just to name a few are all doing unabashedly postmodern work that is free wheeling and exacting in its deployment of emotion. We eventually get there (to the emo place) in Perloff but it's a question of the right feeling which makes me deeply uncomfortable. I think Marjorie's naming of my own transparency has to do with sort of an easy reading of what I do and even missing that it's multiple pronged not single so that I don't clock you with my devices. I surround you and use them. My work has a chameleon quality in which it feels the room and changes. I write to hold the music of the room. If the poet wanders in her studio and that is the text then one can pause while the siren outside blares or even incorporate it into the poem. One of the most important things I know about poetry is that the words don't need to be heard. They aren't ever. Not all of them. And I think of that as an emotional truth. Poems are not made out of words. They're made out of emotional absences, rips and tears. That's the incomplete true fabric of the text.

At the outset of Perloff's original piece she sneers at the "lyric speaker" (supposedly from the other team or stream but maybe me) who "really feels the pain … of the death of a loved one." Which just seems so macho and destructive. In Perloff's universe one needs to access feeling (we'll get to this later) *in an avant garde way*. The difficulty is that when you put it that way it's no longer aesthetics. You're talking about class. When she describes language poetry as having "provided a serious challenge to the *delicate* lyric of self-expression and direct speech …" I feel bad for the limp wristed word *delicate* because it sure takes the hit of Marjorie's contempt. In a bit she will explain for us how she traded up to conceptualism because (sigh) by the 90s language poetry "*felt* [my emphasis] compelled to be more inclusive with respect to gender, race and ethnic diversity," and then, "it became" (exasperated) "difficult to tell *what was* a language poem." With Conceptualism's arrival we have the bracing clarity of Vanessa Place's very untransparent (so Perloff says) *Statement of Facts* which appropriates accounts of sexual violence from Place's work life as a lawyer and which she uses in *Statement of Facts* to "force the reader to revaluate the meaning of seemingly simple propositions" and even begin to "wonder whether we can trust any of the 'factual' statements we are given in police reports and court testimony." And really? Is that what most of us would naturally think about here:

Dorothy C began crying, the man would threaten her again; at some point, he put his mouth on Dorothy C's breasts and neck, and asked her to put his penis in her mouth. She orally copulated him, a minute later, he turned her over and put his penis in her vagina, ejaculating outside the vagina one to five minutes later …

I think it's actually very emotionally evocative and even transparent material and yet the author and the critic's request be that we merely *evaluate* it seems like a seriously traumatized (and privileged [this hasn't happened to me!]) response to these materials. And of course there's the old fashioned use of the word transparent. I mean the traditional mode of conquest of the art or literary world by a woman of every generation is always to use her body sensationally. The naked woman will always find her way in the art world. And after all it is *her* body. Here Vanessa is showing the body she has access to which is the underclass violated body. The worthless body of the victim. I'm not suggesting it's *wrong* of her to do this. I totally get it. But it *feels* wrong somehow. And for me the biggest problem comes when Marjorie reminds us that this work is not transparent. Cause it's both awful in terms of how it feels in the room to hear these materials used that way (I feel violated) and it's transparent in the old fashioned way I began to say earlier which is that "Vanessa's *so* transparent." Sexual violence remains the highroad to success. (This work has a lotta legs.) But back to how it feels "in the room." I mean since one in three women in this country (myself included—fuck here *I* go being transparent again!) have experienced sexual violence I think many readers would have to have a wide variety of responses to these materials rather than being merely "forced to re-evaluate" as one is singularly being instructed to do here. Whose courtroom in what state are we in anyhow. "Feeling" will always interfere with the advised (and really I mean masculine) reading of such texts but feeling (how about we try substituting "being female" for feeling just as a stunt) is always a problem (a good one) in literature and feeling, and if you remember, feeling, i.e. "feeling compelled" was language poetry's (for Perloff) downfall. And still I want to know who or what *was* compelling language poetry to feel that way. The women already in the language poetry room? New Narrative writers in the Bay Area. The fact that people wanted grants or jobs or just realized they *looked* bad. Maybe something great. That's possible. But all of it gets compacted in Perloff's aesthetic (whenever she has to dispense *really* swiftly with "others" she tends to say "and so on" as if unwilling to recite the interminable list of outsiders clamoring) as identity politics or the politically correct. Which is stunning language for a scholar to use. It's media speak. It's transparent speech. Because while not self-identifying one as a sexist, racist or homophobic it does offer a way to speak over the fence to those who *know* what you mean. But what do *you* mean? Do we know? Among language, poetry's sovereign powers Marjorie nostalgically cites: it "demanded an end to transparency." Meaning the refusal of the direct and indirect speech that women and people of color and queers and assorted weaklings of the underclasses have always employed so they don't bump into each other, die of boredom at work or get killed.

Later on when Marjorie discusses the work of Peter Gizzi, Charles Bernstein, and Susan Howe she gets to the point which is that each of these people have undergone recent personal tragedies. And I'm feeling wary (now because I'm about to be told about the avant garde way of mourning. And we've already learned that avant garde poetry might initially exclude certain people, certain kinds of direct statements, certain *bodies* and later by means of appropriation, pastiche all of which everyone has been using for decades but now Marjorie tells us that Conceptual poets are *really* using these tools. Conceptualism I think is the first school of poetry that has appropriated previously known tools (like appropriation) to tear the veils from the eyes of (I guess) of other poets who already knew about these things. Maybe Conceptualism is not for other poets. Conceptualists

(I mean the ones that call themselves that) might finally and actually be making the avant garde accessible to the masses. Because the masses are not about reading and neither is conceptualism. Yay.

Perloff finally holds up three very wonderful poets (who do not claim to be conceptualists, she says) each of them as "an example of the power of *other people's words* to generate profound emotion …" Which is obviously the party that language poetry *could* have hung in for. It's an interesting thought.

When Charles Bernstein's poems verge on bathos (actually they're funny and that jerky excess of "wrong feeling" is for me how they spill over into profound feeling) Perloff claims they are actually recuperated by means of "echo" which is what I think Peter Sloterdijk means by "an amorous bell," a kind of deep connection involving sound that also engages on a compassionate level. Later Peter Gizzi's goofy (goofy good I mean) lyrics are explained in terms that suggest they are a sort of drag. Which would have been a great and gendered way to describe it but why do that when Marjorie can just reach for misogyny instead. The mythic "Echo" in Gizzi's poems is apparently learning to "communicate in *her* restricted state (O Conceptualism!) with far more personal purpose than *her earlier gossiping* …"

The work Marjorie is describing here is important, beautiful and profound. And appropriation has always been the most traditional way to mourn or mark a moment. Most people don't write. And in this writers are people too. We use texts for all our purposes, being human. To illustrate I think of a large reading that took place it seemed only days after 9/11 at St. Mark's Church. There were a wide range of approaches each poet, or performer took when they got up to the podium. Most read somebody else's work. One woman intoned a single note from the back of the church and walked up the center aisle humming with it, only ceasing when she got to the front. She faced us then in silence and it was like she had measured the pain in the room with that one note. It seemed obvious that the shock of what had happened in our city was so huge that hardly anyone had *written* a statement. But everyone could find a text to read that they were feeling through and wanted to share. Each one of the poets Perloff discusses is rising to an occasion similar to what I'm describing here but in their own lives. But I wind up feeling troubled by Marjorie's informing us about the Pygmalion process achieved in conceptual writing where the once womanly transparent feelings are now successfully marshaled into order, stuffed into the echoaic format. The difficulty of reading Perloff's criticism is that the work she's touting is held aloft like these are the poster children for better suffering while Rita Dove's sad marionettes are stupid, the poets in that book *think* they are experiencing suffering, bah! Perloff's dismissiveness feels way other than entirely formal which becomes the problem with her entire argument. Language poetry didn't lose its shit in the 90s because the PC police were banging down the door. Feeling is an inside and outside gong. It's history. But Perloff's busily backing someone out of the lot, rolling in the next ones, shit happens she shrugs, and as informed readers we're supposed to go uh huh and get on with helping her buff up the new statuary. The need for feeling in poetry is of utmost importance to Perloff, but what I come away with is that it's the quality of the feelers (meaning whose) that's the thing most important and true. Which is very postmodern, incredibly elitist, and certainly transparent to boot.

SANCHEZ AND DAY

Robert Glück

One morning I was walking Lily around 29th and Sanchez. Lily, whose motto is better safe than sorry, trotted not too far ahead, avoiding Dobermans and saying hello to pedestrians, gravely accepting their compliments—her gold eyelashes and extravagant tail. A Chevy pickup turned the corner in front of me and I probably looked too hard at the man in the passenger seat, who had a profile. All at once they started yelling "faggot" and "fucking faggot." I had been in a happy mood and with the last of my ebullience I gave them the finger, which I instantly regretted because the truck screeched to a stop and lurched into a three-point turn. There were four, they were laughing and yelling. Lily and I took off. We ran down Sanchez and turned back down the corner of Day along with the truck. One of them missed me with a beer can. They were laughing and driving parallel to us, but then we cut across Day, leapt up a retaining wall and through a cyclone fence by way of a hole I knew about. The fence surrounded a large field where I sometimes walk Lily late at night, giving her an opportunity to roam around a little on her own and enjoy some damp plant and earth smells.

If they didn't separate the advantage was mine since the field had entrances on both sides. I stood in the center on cut grass in San Francisco's expensive daylight; two blocks away bells began swinging toward noon, and they wouldn't attack someone in broad daylight unless of course they would. You'll understand my fear because television has trained us to understand the fear of a running man. I hoped for no police cars; attacking a homosexual is not such a clear-cut offense as, say, stealing a package of processed cheese. The odor of cut grass reminded

me of my mother's childhood in Denver because she always says it reminds her of that. She lived there during the summers with my great-aunt Charlotte, a regal woman who fed the children tubs of strawberries in heavy cream and bakery bread with huge slabs of butter. That was before the days of cholesterol. But Charlotte advocated health food, brown rice and no sugar, which took some independence fifty years ago. She had plenty to spare. I remember after Uncle Harry's funeral the doorbell rang and an immense basket of fruit from Denver was delivered into my mother's hands. The delivery man said very soberly, "Mrs. Isaacs wanted to be especially sure you received this message from her. Wash it before you eat it." Then I recalled my mother's recent phone conversation with Charlotte, who said, "You were such a pretty girl, are you still pretty?" And my mother replied, "Charlotte, I'm pushing sixty."
My mother, who is first and foremost a granddaughter, a daughter, sister, cousin, niece, wife, mother, sister-in-law, aunt and grandmother. So far the incident was nothing much and it had happened fast but with the sluggishness that precedes violence, so I tried to reassure myself with the safety of family memories of childhoods and old ages.

On the other hand, I had ample time to remember Kevin's bashed-in teeth and Bruce getting rousted and then rousted again by the police, and the Halloween when a man yelling "queer" charged Ed and me with a metal pipe; and to recall an acquaintance, hardly a face even, who one day sat on the blue chenille of the couch in my kitchen. He was murdered by someone he brought home, the neighbors saw the killer's face on and off during the night. That's the logical conclusion to this catalogue of betrayals: the murderer takes you when you're naked and expect tenderness and each by agreement is host to the other's vulnerability. The sky clouded over allowing the green, which had been overexposed, to relax into its full color. Recalling these events did not necessarily indicate great extremity, they are not isolated in the way the grammar of sentence and paragraph isolate them. The threat of physical violence makes one part of the whole. College and my literary education agreed that I should see myself as a random conjunction of life's possibilities, certainly an enviable, luxurious point of view. But it's hard to draw on that as a model when four men are chasing you down the street. What life will that model sustain, and when aren't we being chased? The truck circled, pulled over at the entrance on 30th, the men piled out. I waited until they were out of the truck, then exited from the opposite side with Lily keeping close to my legs. Her eyes were dilated; she was vibrant and totally thrilled by the escape. We ran down to Church, turned the corner and slipped into a produce market.

The store was filled with strawberries and the odor of strawberries. I picked two baskets, making sure they were red on the bottom as well as on top, that they weren't moldy, that they smelled strong and healthy. People from Thailand ran the store, and oddly, it seemed to me, they had the country-western music station playing. "Stand by Your Man" by Tammy Wynette, Willie Nelson's intimate version of "Georgia on My Mind," intelligent song—and the Eagles' song that begins by drawing out the beautiful word desperado. Then there was the kind of song I like a lot, where two people exchange verses answering and explaining. He worked on the dayshift and her husband worked on the nightshift. They lived in Pittsburgh and you could call them the Pittsburgh Steelers because, in voices resonant with country-western pain that made the joke dimensional, they stole love and pleasure whenever they got the chance. You might think that I like the song because I identify but that would be wrong. Their love was a child's secret hiding place for chocolate, hidden in the difference between their needs and their lives. It's true that I carry in my spine, wrists and knees the glance of a man I passed three years ago walking up 18th Street, and the shock I felt on seeing that he was completely to my taste. But the difference between these plaintive singers and myself is greater. The difference: walking on 29th a bunch of men in a truck yelled "faggot" at me.

The song ended and then I heard the sound of brakes screeching and then one, two, three, thud!—somebody's in trouble. We looked through the window to see the pickup piled into a telephone pole. A fender was balled up like tinfoil and they stood there wearing uncertain smiles, looking small and bewildered. I picked out the attractive one and when he turned I saw he was holding his hands in front of a mess of blood on his face. I stood a minute, enjoying the sheer pleasure of breathing in and out. I resolved to make my bed, throw away papers, read Gramsci's Prison Notebooks, have an active, no, a famous social life.

Of course that makes for a satisfying if frivolous ending. What really happened was that the men and the truck disappeared except from my imagination. I had angry dreams. Even in my erotic fantasies I couldn't banish a violence that twisted the plot away from pleasure to confusion and fear. And what I resolved was this: that I would gear my writing to tell you about incidents like the one at Sanchez and Day, to put them to you as real questions that need answers, and that these questions, along with my understanding and my practice, would grow more energetic and precise.

THE FISHERWOMAN'S DAUGHTER

Ursula K. Le Guin

I read the first version of this paper at Brown University and at Miami University in Ohio, and revised it heavily to read at Wesleyan College in Georgia. Then I wrote it all over again to read at Portland State University. I have a feeling I read it somewhere else, but can't reconstruct where. When I went to Tulane to be a Mellon Fellow—to be precise, a quarter of a Mellon—I rewrote it again, and that version, which I pretended was definitive, appeared in Tulane's series of Mellon papers, under the title "A Woman Writing." Asked to give the talk in a benefit series in San Francisco, I decided to include more about my mother, whose writing life was lived in the Bay Area; and that led to another full revision.

In preparing the manuscript of this book, I came to the immense folder containing the five—in places identical, in places widely differing—typescripts of the talk; and I thought, "If I have to rewrite that thing once more I will die." So I merely included the latest version, without rereading it. My ruthless editor would have none of that. "Pusillanimous woman," she said, "what about all the bits you left out?" "What about them?" I snarled. "I think if we just put them together it will work," said she. "Show me," said I, craftily. So she did. I hope it does.

What pleases me most about the piece, after so much work on it, is that I can look on it at last as a collaboration. The responses from the various audiences I read it to, both questions in the lecture hall and letters afterward, guided and clarified my thinking and saved me from many follies and omissions. The present re-collation and editing has given me back the whole thing—not shapely and elegant, but a big crazy quilt. And that was my working title for it when I first began gathering material: "Crazy Quilt." That name hints again at collaboration, which is what I saw myself as doing as I pieced together the works and words of so many other writers—ancestors, strangers, friends.

* * *

"'So of course,' wrote Betty Flanders, pressing her heels rather deeper in the sand, 'there was nothing for it but to leave.'"

That is the first sentence of Virginia Woolf's *Jacob's Room*.[1] It is a woman writing. Sitting on the sand by the sea, writing. It's only Betty Flanders, and she's only writing a letter. But first sentences are doors to worlds. This world of Jacob's room, so strangely empty at the end of the book when the mother stands in it holding out a pair of her son's old shoes and saying, "What am I to do with these?"—this is a world in which the first thing one sees is a woman, a mother of children, writing.

On the shore, by the sea, outdoors, is that where women write? Not at a desk, in a writing room? Where does a woman write, what does she look like writing, what is my image, your image, of a woman writing? I asked my friends: "A woman writing: what do you see?" There would be a pause, then the eyes would light up, seeing. Some sent me to paintings, Fragonard, Cassatt, but mostly these turned out to be paintings of a woman reading or with a letter, not actually writing or reading the letter but looking up from it with unfocused eyes: Will he never never

1 Virginia Woolf, *Jacob's Room* (New York: Harcourt Brace Jovanovich, n.d.), 7.

return? Did I remember to turn off the pot roast? … Another friend responded crisply, "A woman writing is taking dictation." And another said, "She's sitting at the kitchen table, and the kids are yelling."

And that last is the image I shall pursue. But first let me tell you my own first answer to my question: Jo March. From the immediacy, the authority, with which Frank Merrill's familiar illustrations of *Little Women* came to my mind as soon as I asked myself what a woman writing looks like, I know that Jo March must have had real influence upon me when I was a young scribbler.[2] I am sure she has influenced many girls, for she is not, like most "real" authors, either dead or inaccessibly famous; nor, like so many artists in books, is she set apart by sensitivity or suffering or general superlativity; nor is she, like most authors in novels, male. She is close as a sister and common as grass. As a model, what does she tell scribbling girls? I think it worthwhile to follow the biography of Jo March the Writer until we come to that person of whom, as a child and until quite recently, I knew almost nothing: Louisa May Alcott.

We first meet Jo as a writer when sister Amy vengefully burns her manuscript, "the loving work of several years. It seemed a small loss to others, but to Jo it was a dreadful calamity." How could a book, several years' work, be "a small loss" to anyone? That horrified me. How could they ask Jo to forgive Amy? At least she nearly drowns her in a frozen lake before forgiving her. At any rate, some chapters later Jo is,

> very busy in the garret … seated on the old sofa, writing busily, with her papers

2 The edition of *Little Women* I used was my mother's and is now my daughter's. It was published in Boston by Little, Brown, undated, around the turn of the century, and Merrill's fine drawings have also been reproduced in other editions.

> spread out on a trunk before her … Jo's desk up here was an old tin kitchen …

—the *OED* says, "New England: a roasting pan." So Jo's room of her own at this stage is a garret furnished with a sofa, a roasting pan, and a rat. To any twelve-year-old, heaven.

> Jo scribbled away till the last page was filled, when she signed her name with a flourish … Lying back on the sofa she read the manuscript carefully through, making dashes here and there, and putting in many exclamation points, which looked like little balloons; then she tied it up with a smart red ribbon and sat a minute looking at it with a sober, wistful expression, which plainly showed how earnest her work had been.

I am interested here by the counter play of a deflating irony—the scribbling, the dashes, the balloons, the ribbon—and that wistful earnestness.

Jo sends her story to a paper, it is printed, and she reads it aloud to her sisters, who cry at the right places. Beth asks, "Who wrote it?"

> The reader suddenly sat up, cast away the paper, displaying a flushed countenance, and with a funny mixture of solemnity and excitement, replied, in a loud voice, "Your sister."

The March family makes a great fuss, "for these foolish, affectionate people made a jubilee of every little household joy"—and there again is deflation, a writer's first publication reduced to a "little household joy." Does it not debase art? And yet does it not also, by refusing the heroic tone, refuse to inflate art into something beyond the reach of any "mere girl"?

So Jo goes on writing; here she is some years later, and I quote at length, for this is the central image.

> Every few weeks she would shut herself up in her room, put on her scribbling suit, and "fall into a vortex," as she expressed it, writing away at her novel with all her heart and soul, for till that was finished she could find no peace. Her "scribbling suit" consisted of a black woollen pinafore on which she could wipe her pen at will, and a cap of the same material, adorned with a cheerful red bow ... This cap was a beacon to the inquiring eyes of her family, who during these periods kept their distance, merely popping in their heads semi-occasionally to ask, with interest, "Does genius burn, Jo?" They did not always venture even to ask this question, but took an observation of the cap, and judged accordingly. If this expressive article of dress was drawn low upon the forehead, it was a sign that hard work was going on; in exciting moments it was pushed rakishly askew; and when despair seized the author it was plucked wholly off and cast upon the floor. At such times the intruder silently withdrew; and not until the red bow was seen gayly erect upon the gifted brow, did anyone dare address Jo.
>
> She did not think herself a genius by any means; but when the writing fit came on, she gave herself up to it with entire abandon, and led a blissful life, unconscious of want, care, or bad weather,

> while she sat safe and happy in an imaginary world, full of friends almost as real and dear to her as any in the flesh. Sleep forsook her eyes, meals stood untasted, day and night were all too short to enjoy the happiness which blessed her only at such times, and made these hours worth living, even if they bore no other fruit. The divine afflatus usually lasted a week or two, and then she emerged from her vortex, hungry, sleepy, cross, or despondent.

This is a good description of the condition in which the work of art is done. This is the real thing—domesticated. The cap and bow, the facetious turns and the disclaimers, deflate without degrading, and allow Alcott to make a rather extraordinary statement: that Jo is doing something very important and doing it entirely seriously and that there is nothing unusual about a young woman's doing it. This passion of work and this happiness which blessed her in doing it are fitted without fuss into a girl's commonplace life at home. It may not seem much; but I don't know where else I or many other girls like me, in my generation or my mother's or my daughters', were to find this model, this validation.

Jo writes romantic thrillers and they sell; her father shakes his head and says, "Aim at the highest and never mind the money," but Amy remarks, "The money is the best part of it." Working in Boston as a governess-seamstress, Jo sees that "money conferred power: money and power, therefore, she resolved to have; not to be used for herself alone," our author's author hastily adds, "but for those whom she loved more than self … She took to writing sensation stories." Her first visit to the editorial office of the *Weekly Volcano* is handled lightly, but the three men treat her as a woman who has come to sell herself—true Lévi-Straussians, to whom what a woman does is entirely subsumed in woman as commodity. Refusing shame, Jo writes on, and makes money by her writing; admitting shame, she does not "tell them at home."

> Jo soon found that her innocent experience had given her but few glimpses of the tragic world which underlies society; so, regarding it in a business light, she set about supplying her deficiencies with characteristic energy ... She searched newspapers for accidents, incidents, and crimes; she excited the suspicions of public librarians by asking for works on poisons; she studied faces in the street, and characters good, bad, and indifferent all about her ... Much describing of other people's passions and feelings set her to studying and speculating about her own—a morbid amusement, in which healthy young minds do not voluntarily indulge—

but which one might think appropriate, even needful, to the young novelist? However, "wrongdoing always brings its own punishment, and when Jo most needed hers, she got it."

Her punishment is administered by the Angel in the House, in the form of Professor Bhaer. Knowing that she is soiling her pure soul, he attacks the papers she writes for: "I do not like to think that good young girls should see such things." Jo weakly defends them, but when he leaves she rereads her stories, three months' work, and burns them. Amy doesn't have to do it for her any more; she can destroy herself. Then she sits and wonders: "I almost wish I hadn't any conscience, it's so inconvenient!" A cry from the heart of Bronson Alcott's daughter. She tries a pious tale and a children's story, which don't sell, and gives up: she "corked up her inkstand."

Beth dies, and trying to replace her, Jo tries "to live for others"—finally driving her mother to say, "Why don't you write? That always used to make you happy." So she does, and she writes both well and successfully—until Professor Bhaer returns and marries her, evidently the only way to make her stop writing. She has his two boys to bring up, and then her two boys, and then all those Little Men in the next volume; at the end of *Little Women*, in the chapter called "Harvest Time," she says, "I haven't given up the hope that I may write a good book yet, but I can wait."

The harvest seems indefinitely deferred. But, in Rachel Blau DuPlessis' phrase, Jo writes beyond the ending. In the third volume, *Jo's Boys*, she has gone back in middle age to writing, and is rich and famous.[3] There is realism, toughness, and comedy in the descriptions of her managing the household, mothering the teenagers, writing her chapters, and trying to avoid the celebrity hunters. In fact this, like the whole story of Jo the Writer, is quite close to Louisa Alcott's own story, with one large difference. Jo marries and has children. Lu did not.

And yet she undertook the responsibility for a family, some of whom were as improvident and self-centered as any baby. There is a heartbreaking note in her journal for April 1869, when she was suffering a "bad spell" of mercury poisoning (the calomel given her to cure fever when she was a nurse in the Civil War made her sick the rest of her life):

3 See Rachel Blau DuPlessis, *Writing Beyond the Ending: Narrative Strategies of Twentieth-Century Women Writers* (Bloomington: Indiana University Press, 1985).

> Very poorly. Feel quite used up. Don't care much for myself, as rest is heavenly, even with pain; but the family seems so panic-stricken and helpless when I break down, that I try to keep the mill going. Two short tales for L., $50; two for Ford, $20; and did my editorial work, though two months are unpaid for. Roberts wants a new book, but am afraid to get into a vortex lest I fall ill.[4]

Alcott used the same word Jo used for her passions of writing; here are a couple of journal passages comparable to the "vortex" passage in *Little Women*.

> August 1860—"Moods" [a novel]. Genius burned so fiercely that for four weeks I wrote all day and planned nearly all night, being quite possessed by my work. I was perfectly happy, and seemed to have no wants.
>
> February 1861—Another turn at "Moods," which I remodelled. From the 2nd to the 25th I sat writing, with a run at dusk; could not sleep, and for three days was so full of it I could not stop to get up. Mother made me a green silk cap with a red bow, to match the old green and red party wrap, which I wore as a "glory cloak."
>
> Thus arrayed sat in a grove of manuscripts, "living for immortality" as May

4 Louisa May Alcott, *Life, Letters, and Journals* (Boston: Roberts Brothers, 1890). The passages quoted are on pages 203, 122, and 125.

> said. Mother wandered in and out with cordial cups of tea, worried because I couldn't eat. Father thought it fine, and brought his reddest apples and hardest cider for my Pegasus to feed upon … It was very pleasant and queer while it lasted …

And it is pleasant to see how the family whose debts she slaved to pay off, and which she strove so to protect and keep in comfort, tried to protect and help her in return.

Like so many women of her century, then, Lu Alcott had a family, though she did not marry. "Liberty is a better husband than love to many of us," she wrote, but in fact she had very little liberty, in the sense of freedom from immediate, personal responsibilities. She even had a baby—her sister May's. Dying from complications of childbirth, May asked the beloved older sister, then forty-eight, to bring up little Lu; which she did until her death eight years later.

All this is complex, more complex, I think, than one tends to imagine; for the Victorian script calls for a clear choice—either books or babies for a woman, not both. And Jo *seems* to make that choice. I was annoyed at myself when I realized that I had forgotten Jo's survival as a writer—that my memory, except for one nagging scrap that led me to look up *Jo's Boys* at last, had followed the script. That, of course, is the power of the script: you play the part without knowing it.

Here is a classic—a scriptural—description of a writing woman, the mother of children, one of whom is just now in the process of falling down the stairs.

> Mrs. Jellyby was a pretty, very diminutive, plump woman, of from forty to fifty, with handsome eyes, though they had a curious

> habit of seeming to look a long way off … [She] had very good hair, but was too much occupied with her African duties to brush it … We could not help noticing that her dress didn't nearly meet up the back, and that the open space was railed across with a latticework of stay-laces—like a summer-house.
>
> The room, which was strewn with papers and nearly filled by a great writing-table covered with similar litter, was, I must say, not only very untidy, but very dirty. We were obliged to take notice of that with our sense of sight, even while, with our sense of hearing, we followed the poor child who had tumbled downstairs: I think into the back kitchen, where somebody seemed to stifle him. But what principally struck us was a jaded and unhealthy-looking, though by no means plain girl, at the writing-table, who sat biting the feather of her pen, and staring at us. I suppose nobody ever was in such a state of ink.[5]

I will, with difficulty, restrain myself from reading you the rest of *Bleak House*. I love Dickens and will defend his Mrs. Jellyby and her correspondence with Borrioboola-Gha as an eternal send-up of those who meddle with foreign morals while remaining oblivious to the misery under their nose. But I observe also that he uses a woman to make this point, probably because it was, and is, safe: few readers would

5 Charles Dickens, *Bleak House* (New York: Thomas Y. Crowell, n.d.), 41.

question the assumption that a woman should put family before public responsibility, or that if she does work outside the "private sphere" she will be neglectful of her house, indifferent to the necks of her children, and incompetent to fasten her clothing. Mrs. Jellyby's daughter is saved from her enforced "state of ink" by marriage, but Mrs. Jellyby will get no help from her husband, a man so inert that their marriage is described as the union of mind and matter. Mrs. Jellyby is a joy to me, she is drawn with so much humor and good nature; and yet she troubles me, because behind her lurks the double standard. Nowhere among Dickens' many responsible, intelligent women is there one who does real artistic or intellectual work, to balance Mrs. Jellyby and reassure us that it isn't what she does but how she does it that is deplorable. And yet the passage just quoted is supposed to have been written by a woman—the character Esther Summerson. Esther herself is a problem. How does she write half Dickens' novel for him while managing Bleak House and getting smallpox and everything else? We never catch her at it. As a woman writing, Esther is invisible. She is not in the script.

There may be a sympathetic portrait of a woman writer with children in a novel written by a man. I have read versions of this paper in Rhode Island, Ohio, Georgia, Louisiana, Oregon, and California, and asked each audience please to tell me if they knew of any such. I wait in hope. Indeed, the only sympathetic picture of a woman novelist in a man's novel that I know is the protagonist of *Diana of the Crossways*. Meredith shows her writing novels for her living, doing it brilliantly, and finding her freedom in her professionalism. But, self-alienated by a disastrous infatuation, she begins to force her talent and can't work—the script apparently being that love is incidental for a man, everything for a woman. At the end, well off and happily married, she is expecting a baby, but not, it appears, a book. All the same, Diana still stands, nearly a century later, quite alone at her crossways.

Invisibility as a writer is a condition that affects not only characters but authors, and even the children of authors. Take Elizabeth Barrett Browning, whom we have consistently put to bed with a spaniel, ignoring the fact that when she wrote *Aurora Leigh* she was the healthy mother of a healthy four-year-old—ignoring, in fact, the fact that she wrote *Aurora Leigh*, a book about being a woman writer, and how difficult one's own true love can make it for one.

Here is a woman who had several children and was a successful novelist, writing a letter to her husband about a hundred and fifty years ago, or maybe last night:

> If I *am* to write, I must have a room to myself, which shall be *my* room. All last winter I felt the need of some place where I could go and be quiet. I could not [write in the dining room] for there was all the setting of tables and clearing up of tables and dressing and washing of children, and everything else going on, and … I never felt comfortable there, though I tried hard. Then if I came into the parlor where you were, I felt as if I were interrupting you, and you know you sometimes thought so too.[6]

What do you mean? Not at all! Silly notion! Just like a woman!

6 Harriet Beecher Stowe, 1841, quoted in Tillie Olsen, *Silences* (New York: Dell, Laurel Editions, 1983), 227.

Fourteen years and several more children later, that woman wrote *Uncle Tom's Cabin*—most of it at the kitchen table.

A room of one's own—yes. One may ask why Mr. Harriet Beecher Stowe got a room to himself to write in, while the woman who wrote the most morally effective American novel of the nineteenth century got the kitchen table. But then one may also ask why she accepted the kitchen table. Any self-respecting man would have sat there for five minutes and then stalked out shouting, "Nobody can work in this madhouse, call me when dinner's ready!" But Harriet, a self-respecting woman, went on getting dinner with the kids all underfoot *and* writing her novels. The first question, to be asked with awe, is surely, How? But then, Why? *Why* are women such patsies?

The quick-feminist-fix answer is that they are victims of and/or accomplices with the patriarchy, which is true but doesn't really get us anywhere new. Let us go to another woman novelist for help. I stole the Stowe quotation (and others) from Tillie Olsen's *Silences*, a book to which this paper stands in the relation of a loving but undutiful daughter—Hey, Ma, that's a neat quotation, can I wear it? This next one I found for myself, in the *Autobiography* of Margaret Oliphant, a fascinating book, from the generation just after Stowe. Oliphant was a successful writer very young, married, had three kids, went on writing, was left a widow with heavy debts and the three kids plus her brother's three kids to bring up, did so, went on writing ... When her second book came out, she was still, like Jo March, a girl at home.

> I had a great pleasure in writing, but the success and the three editions had no particular effect upon my mind ... I had nobody to praise me except my mother and [brother] Frank, and their applause—

> well, it was delightful, it was everything in the world—it was life—but it did not count. They were part of me, and I of them, and we were all in it.[7]

I find that extraordinary. I cannot imagine any male author saying anything like that at all. There is a key here—something real that has been neglected, been hidden, been denied.

> ... The writing ran through everything. But then it was also subordinate to everything, to be pushed aside for any little necessity. I had no table even to myself, much less a room to work in, but sat at the corner of the family table with my writing-book, with everything going on as if I had been making a shirt instead of writing a book ... My mother sat always at needlework of some kind, and talked to whoever might be present, and I took my share in the conversation, going on all the same with my story, the little groups of imaginary persons, these other talks evolving themselves quite undisturbed.

How's that for an image, the group of imaginary people talking in the imaginary room in the real room among the real people talking, and all of it going on perfectly quiet and unconfused ... But it's shocking. She can't be a real writer. Real writers writhe on solitary sofas in cork-lined rooms, agonizing after *le mot juste*—don't they?

7 This and the subsequent connected passages are from the *Autobiography and Letters of Mrs. Margaret Oliphant*, edited by Mrs. Harry Coghill (Leicester: Leicester University Press, The Victorian Library, 1974), 23–24.

> My study, all the study I have ever attained to, is the little second drawing-room where all the life of the house goes on …

—you recall that she was bringing up six children?—

> … and I don't think I have ever had two hours undisturbed (except at night when everybody is in bed) during my whole literary life. Miss Austen, I believe, wrote in the same way, and very much for the same reason; but at her period the natural flow of life took another form. The family were half ashamed to have it known that she was not just a young lady like the others, doing her embroidery. Mine were quite pleased to magnify me and to be proud of my work, but always with a hidden sense that it was an admirable joke …

—perhaps artists cast off their families and go to the South Sea Islands because they want to be perceived as heroes and their families think they are funny?—

> … a hidden sense that it was an admirable joke, and no idea that any special facilities or retirement was necessary. My mother would have felt her pride much checked, almost humiliated, if she had conceived that I stood in need of any artificial aids of that description. That would at once have made the work unnatural to her eyes, and also to mine.

Oliphant was a proud Scotswoman, proud of her work and her strength; yet she wrote nonfiction potboilers rather than fight her male editors and publishers for better pay for her novels. So, as she says bitterly, "Trollope's worst book was better paid than my best." Her best is said to be *Miss Marjoribanks*, but I have never yet been able to get a copy of it; it was disappeared, along with all her other books. Thanks to publishers such as Virago we can now get Oliphant's *Hester*, a stunning novel, and *Kirsteen* and a few others, but they are still taught, so far as I know, only in women's studies courses; they are not part of the Canon of English Literature, though Trollope's potboilers are. No book by a woman who had children has ever been included in that august list.

I think Oliphant gives us a glimpse of why a novelist might not merely endure writing in the kitchen or the parlor amidst the children and the housework, but might endure it willingly. She seems to feel that she

profited, that her writing profited, from the difficult, obscure, chancy connection between the art work and the emotional/manual/managerial complex of skills and tasks called "housework," and that to sever that connection would put the writing itself at risk, would make it, in her word, unnatural.

The received wisdom of course is just the opposite: that any attempt to combine art work with housework and family responsibility is impossible, unnatural. And the punishment for unnatural acts, among the critics and the Canoneers, is death.

What is the ethical basis of this judgment and sentence upon the housewife-artist? It is a very noble and austere one, with religion at its foundation: it is the idea that the artist must sacrifice himself to his art. (I use the pronoun advisedly.) His responsibility is to his work alone. It is a motivating idea of the Romantics, it guides the careers of poets from Rimbaud to Dylan Thomas to Richard Hugo, it has given us hundreds of hero figures, typical of whom is

James Joyce himself and his Stephen Dedalus. Stephen sacrifices all "lesser" obligations and affections to a "higher" cause, embracing the moral irresponsibility of the soldier or the saint. This heroic stance, the Gauguin Pose, has been taken as the norm—as natural to the artist—and artists, both men and women, who do not assume it have tended to feel a little shabby and second-rate.

Not, however, Virginia Woolf. She observed factually that the artist needs a small income and a room to work in, but did not speak of heroism. Indeed, she said, "I doubt that a writer can be a hero. I doubt that a hero can be a writer." And when I see a writer assume the full heroic posture, I incline to agree. Here, for example, is Joseph Conrad:

> For twenty months I wrestled with the Lord for my creation … mind and will and conscience engaged to the full, hour after hour, day after day … a lonely struggle in a great isolation from the world. I suppose I slept and ate the food put before me and talked connectedly on suitable occasions, but I was never aware of the even flow of daily life, made easy and noiseless for me by a silent, watchful, tireless affection.[8]

A woman who boasted that her conscience had been engaged to the full in such a wrestling match would be called to account by both women and men; and women are now calling men to account. What "put food" before him? What made daily life so noiseless? What in fact was this "tireless affection," which sounds to me like an old Ford in a junkyard but is apparently intended as a delicate gesture towards a woman whose conscience was engaged to the full,

8 Joseph Conrad, quoted in Olsen, 30.

hour after hour, day after day, for twenty months, in seeing to it that Joseph Conrad could wrestle with the Lord in a very relatively great isolation, well housed, clothed, bathed, and fed?

Conrad's "struggle" and Jo March/Lu Alcott's "vortex" are descriptions of the same kind of all-out artistic work; and in both cases the artist is looked after by the family. But I feel an important difference in their perceptions. Where Alcott receives a gift, Conrad asserts a right; where she is taken into the vortex, the creative whirlwind, becoming part of it, he wrestles, struggles, seeking mastery. She is a participant; he is a hero. And her family remain individuals, with cups of tea and timid inquiries, while his is depersonalized to "an affection."

Looking for a woman writer who might have imitated this heroic infantilism, I thought of Gertrude Stein, under the impression that she had used Alice

Toklas as a "wife" in this utilitarian sense; but that, as I should have guessed, is an anti-lesbian canard. Stein certainly took hero-artist poses and indulged an enormous ego, but she played fair; and the difference between her domestic partnership and that of Joyce or Conrad is illuminating. And indeed, lesbianism has given many artists the network of support they need—for there *is* a heroic aspect to the practice of art; it is lonely, risky, merciless work, and every artist needs some kind of moral support or sense of solidarity and validation.

The artist with the least access to social or aesthetic solidarity or approbation has been the artist-housewife. A person who undertakes responsibility both to her art and to her dependent children, with no "tireless affection" or even tired affection to call on, has undertaken a full-time double job that can be simply, practically, destroyingly impossible. But that isn't how the problem is posed—as a recognition of immense practical difficulty. If it were, practical solutions would be proposed, beginning with childcare. Instead the issue is stated, even now, as a moral one, a matter of ought and ought not. The poet Alicia Ostriker puts it neatly: "That women should have babies rather than books is the considered opinion of Western civilization. That women should have books rather than babies is a variation on that theme."[9]

Freud's contribution to this doctrine was to invest it with such a weight of theory and mythology as to make it appear a primordial, unquestionable fact. It was of course Freud who, after telling his fiancée what it is a woman wants, said that what we shall never know is what a woman wants. Lacan is perfectly consistent in following him, if I as a person without discourse may venture to say so. A culture or a psychology predicated upon man as human and woman as other cannot accept a woman as artist. An artist is an autonomous, choice-making self: to be such a self a woman must unwoman herself. Barren, she must imitate the man—imperfectly, it goes without saying.*

Hence the approbation accorded Austen, the Brontes, Dickinson, and Plath, who though she made the mistake of having two children compensated for it by killing herself. The misogynist Canon of Literature can include these women because they can be perceived as incomplete women, as female men.

Still, I have to grit my teeth to criticize the either-books-or-babies doctrine, because it has given real, true comfort to women who could not or chose not to marry and have children, and saw themselves as "having" books instead. But though the comfort may be real, I think the doctrine false. And I hear that falseness when a Dorothy Richardson tells us that other women can have children but nobody else can

9 Alicia Ostriker, *Writing Like a Woman*, Michigan Poets on Poetry Series (Ann Arbor: University of Michigan Press, 1983), 126.

write *her* books. As if "other women" could have had *her* children—as if books came from the uterus! That's just the flip side of the theory that books come from the scrotum. This final reduction of the notion of sublimation is endorsed by our chief macho dodo writer, who has announced that "the one thing a writer needs to have is balls." But he doesn't carry the theory of penile authorship to the extent of saying that if you "get" a kid you can't "get" a book and so fathers can't write. The analogy collapsed into identity, the you-can't-create-if-you-procreate myth, is applied to women only.

I've found I have to stop now and say clearly what I'm not saying. I'm not saying a writer ought to have children, I'm not saying a parent ought to be a writer, I'm not saying any woman *ought* to write books *or* have kids. Being a mother is one of the things a woman can do—like being a writer. It's a privilege. It's not an obligation, or a destiny. I'm talking about mothers who write because it is almost a taboo topic—because women have been told that they *ought not* to try to be both a mother and a writer because both the kids and the books will *pay*—because it can't be done—because it is unnatural.

* A particularly exhilarating discussion of this issue is the essay "Writing and Motherhood" by Susan Rubin Suleiman, in *The (M)other Tongue: Essays in Feminist Psychoanalytic Interpretation*, ed. Shirley Nelson Garner, Claire Kahane, and Madelon Sprengnether (Ithaca: Cornell University Press, 1985). Suleiman gives a short history of the nineteenth-century books-or-babies theory and its refinement in the twentieth century by such psychologists as Helene Deutsch, remarking that "it took psychoanalysis to transform moral obligation into a psychological 'law,' equating the creative impulse with the procreative one and decreeing that she who has a child feels no need to write books." Suleiman presents a critique of the feminist reversal of this theory (she who has a book feels no need to have children) and analyzes current French feminist thinking on the relationship between writing and femininity/motherhood.

This refusal to allow both creation and procreation to women is cruelly wasteful: not only has it impoverished our literature by banning the housewives, but it has caused unbearable personal pain and self-mutilation: Woolf obeying the wise doctors who said she must not bear a child; Plath who put glasses of milk by her kids' beds and then put her head in the oven.

A sacrifice, not of somebody else but of oneself, is demanded of women artists (while the Gauguin Pose demands of men artists only that they sacrifice others). I am proposing that this ban on a woman artist's full sexuality is harmful not only to the woman but to the art.

There is less censure now, and more support, for a woman who wants both to bring up a family and work as an artist. But it's a small degree of improvement. The difficulty of trying to be responsible, hour after hour day after day for maybe twenty years, for the well-being of children and the excellence of books, is immense: it involves an endless expense of energy and an impossible weighing of competing priorities. And we don't know much about the process, because writers who are mothers haven't talked much about their motherhood—for fear of boasting? for fear of being trapped in the Mom trap, discounted? —nor have they talked much about their writing as in any way connected with their parenting, since the heroic myth demands that the two jobs be considered utterly opposed and mutually destructive.

But we heard a hint of something else from Oliphant; and here (thanks, Tillie) is the painter Käthe Kollwitz:

> I am gradually approaching the period in my life when work comes first. When both the boys were away for Easter, I hardly did anything but work. Worked, slept, ate,

> and went for short walks. But above all I worked.
>
> And yet I wonder whether the "blessing" isn't missing from such work. No longer diverted by other emotions, I work the way a cow grazes.

That is marvelous—"I work the way a cow grazes." That is the best description of the "professional" at work I know.

> Perhaps in reality I accomplish a little more. The hands work and work, and the head imagines it's producing God knows what, and yet, formerly, when my working time was so wretchedly limited, I was more productive, because I was more sensual; I lived as a human being must live, passionately interested in every-

> thing … Potency, potency is diminishing.[10]

This *potency* felt by a woman is a potency from which the Hero-Artist has (and I choose my words carefully) cut himself off, in an egoism that is ultimately sterile. But it is a potency that has been denied by women as well as men, and not just women eager to collude with misogyny.

Back in the seventies Nina Auerbach wrote that Jane Austen was able to write because she had created around her "a child-free space." Germ-free I knew, odor-free I knew, but child-free? And Austen? who wrote in the parlor, and was a central figure to a lot of nieces and nephews? But I tried to accept what Auerbach said, because although my experience didn't fit it, I was, like many women, used to feeling

10 Käthe Kollwitz, Diaries and Letters, quoted in Olsen, 235–36.

that my experience was faulty, not right—that it was *wrong*. So I was probably wrong to keep on writing in what was then a fully child-filled space. However, feminist thinking evolved rapidly to a far more complex and realistic position, and I, stumbling along behind, have been enabled by it to think a little for myself.

The greatest enabler for me was always, is always, Virginia Woolf. And I quote now from the first draft of her paper "Professions for Women,"[11] where she gives her great image of a woman writing.

> I figure her really in an attitude of contemplation, like a fisherwoman, sitting on the bank of a lake with her fishing rod held over its water. Yes that is how I see her. She was not thinking; she was not reasoning; she was not constructing a plot; she was letting her imagination down into the depths of her consciousness while she sat above holding on by a thin but quite necessary thread of reason.

Now I interrupt to ask you to add one small element to this scene. Let us imagine that a bit farther up the bank of the lake sits a child, the fisherwoman's daughter. She's about five, and she's making people out of sticks and mud and telling stories with them. She's been told to be very quiet please while Mama fishes, and she really is very quiet except when she forgets and sings or asks questions; and she watches in fascinated silence when the following dramatic

11 The talk, known in its revised form as "Professions for Women" and so titled in the Essays, was given on January 21, 1931, to the London National Society for Women's Service, and can be found complete with all deletions and alternate readings in Mitchell Leaska's editing of Woolf's *The Pargiters* (New York: Harcourt Brace Jovanovich, 1978).

events take place. There sits our woman writing, our fisherwoman, when—

> suddenly there is a violent jerk; she feels the line race through her fingers.
>
> The imagination has rushed away; it has taken to the depths; it has sunk heaven knows where—into the dark pool of extraordinary experience. The reason has to cry "Stop!" the novelist has to pull on the line and haul the imagination to the surface. The imagination comes to the top in a state of fury.
>
> Good heavens she cries—how dare you interfere with me—how dare you pull me out with your wretched little fishing line? And I—that is, the reason—have to reply, "My dear you were going altogether too far. Men would be shocked." Calm yourself I say, as she sits panting on the bank—panting with rage and disappointment. We have only got to wait fifty years or so. In fifty years I shall be able to use all this very queer knowledge that you are ready to bring me. But not now. You see I go on, trying to calm her, I cannot make use of what you tell me—about women's bodies for instance—their passions—and so on, because the conventions are still very strong. If I were to overcome the conventions I should need the courage of a hero, and I am not a hero.

I doubt that a writer can be a hero.
I doubt that a hero can be a writer.

... Very well, says the imagination, dressing herself up again in her petticoat and skirts, we will wait. We will wait another fifty years. But it seems to me a pity.

It seems to me a pity. It seems to me a pity that more than fifty years have passed and the conventions, though utterly different, still exist to protect men from being shocked, still admit only male experience of women's bodies, passions, and existence. It seems to me a pity that so many women, including myself, have accepted this denial of their own experience and narrowed their perception to fit it, writing as if their sexuality were limited to copulation, as if they knew nothing about pregnancy, birth, nursing, mothering, puberty, menstruation, menopause, except what men are willing to hear, nothing except what men are willing to hear about housework, childwork, lifework, war, peace, living, and dying as experienced in the female body and mind and imagination. "Writing the body," as Woolf asked and Hélène Cixous asks, is only the beginning. We have to rewrite the world.

White writing, Cixous calls it, writing in milk, in mother's milk. I like that image, because even among feminists, the woman writer has been more often considered in her sexuality as a lover than in her sexuality as pregnant-bearing-nursing-childcaring. Mother still tends to get disappeared. And in losing the artist-mother we lose where there's a lot to gain. Alicia Ostriker thinks so. "The advantage of motherhood for a woman artist," she says—have you ever heard anybody say that before? the *advantage* of motherhood for an artist?—

> The advantage of motherhood for a woman artist is that it puts her in immediate and inescapable contact with the sources of life, death, beauty, growth, corruption … If the woman artist has been trained to believe that the activities of motherhood are trivial, tangential to the

> main issues of life, irrelevant to the great themes of literature, she should untrain herself. The training is misogynist, it protects and perpetuates systems of thought and feeling which prefer violence and death to love and birth, and it is a lie.
>
> … "We think back through our mothers, if we are women," declares Woolf, but through whom can those who are themselves mothers … do their thinking? … we all need data, we need information, … the sort provided by poets, novelists, artists, from within. As our knowledge begins to accumulate, we can imagine what it would signify to all women, and men, to live in a culture where childbirth and mothering occupied the kind of position that sex and romantic love have occupied in literature and art for the last five hundred years, or … that warfare has occupied since literature began.[12]

My book *Always Coming Home* was a rash attempt to imagine such a world, where the Hero and the Warrior are a stage adolescents go through on their way to becoming responsible human beings, where the parent-child relationship is not forever viewed through the child's eyes but includes the reality of the mother's experience. The imagining was difficult, and rewarding.

Here is a passage from a novel where what Woolf, Cixous, and Ostriker ask for is happening, however casually and unpretentiously. In Margaret Drabble's *The Millstone*, Rosamund, a young scholar and freelance writer, has a baby about eight months old,

12 Ostriker, 131.

Octavia.[13] They share a flat with a friend, Lydia, who's writing a novel. Rosamund is working away on a book review:

> I had just written and counted my first hundred words when I remembered Octavia; I could hear her making small happy noises …
>
> I was rather dismayed when I realized she was in Lydia's room and that I must have left the door open, for Lydia's room was always full of nasty objects like aspirins, safety razors and bottles of ink; I rushed along to rescue her and the sight that met my eyes when I opened the door was enough to make anyone quake. She had her back to the door and was sitting in the middle of the floor surrounded by a sea of torn, strewed, chewed paper. I stood there transfixed, watching the neat small back of her head and her thin stalk-like neck and flowery curls: suddenly she gave a great screech of delight and ripped another sheet of paper. "Octavia," I said in horror, and she started guiltily, and looked round at me with a charming deprecating smile: her mouth, I could see, was wedged full of wads of Lydia's new novel.
>
> I picked her up and fished the bits out and laid them carefully on the bedside table with what was left of the typescript; pages 70 to 123 seemed to have survived. The rest was in varying stages

13 Margaret Drabble, *The Millstone* (New York: NAL, Plume Books, 1984), 122–23. Also published under the title *Thank You All Very Much*.

> of dissolution: some pages were entire but badly crumpled, some were in large pieces, some in small pieces, and some, as I have said, were chewed up. The damage was not, in fact, as great as it appeared at first sight to be, for babies, though persistent, are not thorough: but at first sight it was frightful … In a way it was clearly the most awful thing for which I had ever been responsible, but as I watched Octavia crawl around the sitting room looking for more work to do, I almost wanted to laugh. It seemed so absurd, to have this small living extension of myself, so dangerous, so vulnerable, for whose injuries and crimes I alone had to suffer … It really was a terrible thing … and yet in comparison with Octavia being so sweet and so alive it did not seem so very terrible …

Confronted with the wreckage, Lydia is startled, but not deeply distressed:

> … and that was it, except for the fact that Lydia really did have to rewrite two whole chapters as well as doing a lot of boring sellotaping, and when it came out it got bad reviews anyway. This did succeed in making Lydia angry.

I have seen Drabble's work dismissed with the usual list of patronizing adjectives reserved for women who write as women, not imitation men. Let us not let her be disappeared. Her work is deeper than its bright surface. What is she talking about in this funny passage? Why does the girl-baby eat not her mother's manuscript but another woman's manuscript?

Couldn't she at least have eaten a manuscript by a man?—no, no, that's not the point. The point, or part of it, is that babies eat manuscripts. They really do. The poem not written because the baby cried, the novel put aside because of a pregnancy, and so on. Babies eat books. But they spit out wads of them that can be taped back together; and they are only babies for a couple of years, while writers live for decades; and it is terrible, but not very terrible. The manuscript that got eaten *was* terrible; if you know Lydia you know the reviewers were right. And that's part of the point too—that the supreme value of art depends on "other equally supreme values. But that subverts the hierarchy of values; "men would be shocked ..."

In Drabble's comedy of morals the absence of the Hero-Artist is a strong ethical statement. Nobody lives in a great isolation, nobody sacrifices human claims, nobody even scolds the baby. Nobody is going to put their head, or anybody else's head, into an oven: not the mother, not the writer, not the daughter—these three and one who, being women, do not separate creation and destruction into *I create / You are destroyed*, or vice versa. Who are responsible, take responsibility, for both the baby and the book.[**] But I want now to turn from fiction to

[**] My understanding of this issue has been very much aided by Carol Gilligan's *In a Different Voice* (Cambridge: Harvard University Press, 1982), as well as by Jean Baker Miller's modestly revolutionary *Toward a New Psychology of Women* (Boston: Beacon Press, 1976). Gilligan's thesis, stated very roughly, is that our society brings up males to think and speak in terms of their rights, females in terms of their responsibilities, and that conventional psychologies have implicitly evaluated the "male" image of a hierarchy of rights as "superior" (hierarchically, of course) to the "female" image of a network of mutual responsibilities. Hence a man finds it (relatively) easy to assert his "right" to be free of relationships and dependents, à la Gauguin, while women are not granted and do not grant one another any such right, preferring to live as part of an intense and

biography and from general to personal; I want to talk a bit about my mother, the writer.

Her maiden name was Theodora Kracaw; her first married name was Brown; her second married name, Kroeber, was the one she used on her books; her third married name was Quinn. This sort of many-namedness doesn't happen to men; it's inconvenient, and yet its very cumbersomeness reveals, perhaps, the being of a woman writer as not one simple thing—the author—but a multiple, complex process of being, with various responsibilities, one of which is to her writing.

Theodora put her personal responsibilities first—chronologically. She brought up and married off her four children before she started to write. She took up the pen, as they used to say—she had the most amazing left-handed scrawl—in her mid-fifties. I asked her once, years later, "Did you want to write, and put it off intentionally, till you'd got rid of us?" And she laughed and said, "Oh, no, I just wasn't *ready*." Not an evasion or a dishonest answer, but not, I think, the whole answer.

She was born in 1897 in a wild Colorado mining town, and her mother boasted of having been *born* with the vote—in Wyoming, which ratified woman suffrage along with statehood—and rode a stallion men couldn't ride; but still, the Angel in the House was very active in those days, the one whose message is that a woman's needs come after everybody else's. And my mother really came pretty close to incarnating that Angel, whom Woolf called "the woman men wish women to be." Men fell in love with her—all men.

complex network in which freedom is arrived at, if at all, mutually. Coming at the matter from this angle, one can see why there are no or very few "Great Artists" among women, when the "Great Artist" is defined as inherently superior to and not responsible towards others.

Doctors, garage mechanics, professors, roach exterminators. Butchers saved sweetbreads for her. She was also, to her daughter, a demanding, approving, nurturing, good-natured, loving, lively mother—a first-rate mother. And then, getting on to sixty, she became a first-rate writer.

She started out, as women so often do, by writing some books for children—not competing with men, you know, staying in the "domestic sphere." One of these, *A Green Christmas*, is a lovely book that ought to be in every six-year-old's stocking. Then she wrote a charming and romantic autobiographical novel—still on safe, "womanly" ground. Next she ventured into Native American territory with *The Inland Whale*; and then she was asked to write the story of an Indian called Ishi, the only survivor of a people massacred by the North American pioneers, a serious and risky subject requiring a great deal of research, moral sensitivity, and organizational and narrative skill.

So she wrote it, the first best seller, I believe, that University of California Press ever published. *Ishi* is still in print in many languages, still used, I think, in California schools, still deservedly beloved. It is a book entirely worthy of its subject, a book of very great honesty and power.

So, if she could write that in her sixties, what might she have written in her thirties? Maybe she really "wasn't ready." But maybe she listened to the wrong angel, and we might have had many more books from her. Would my brothers and I have suffered, have been cheated of anything, if she had been writing them? I think my aunt Betsy and the household help we had back then would have kept things going just fine. As for my father, I don't see how her writing could have hurt him or how her success could have threatened him. But I don't know. All I do know is that once she started writing (and it was while my father was alive, and they collaborated on a couple of things), she never stopped; she had found the work she loved.

Once, not long after my father's death, when *Ishi* was bringing her the validation of praise and success she very much needed, and while I was still getting every story I sent out rejected with monotonous regularity, she burst into tears over my latest rejection slip and tried to console me, saying that she wanted rewards and success for me, not for herself. And that was lovely, and I treasured her saying it then as I do now. That she didn't really mean it and I didn't really believe it made no difference. Of course she didn't want to sacrifice her achievement, her work, to me—why on earth should she? She shared what she could of it with me by sharing the pleasures and anguishes of writing, the intellectual excitement, the shoptalk—and that's all. No angelic altruism. When I began to publish, we shared that. And she wrote on; in her eighties she told me, without bitterness, "I wish

I had started sooner. Now there isn't time." She was at work on a third novel when she died.

As for myself: I have flagrantly disobeyed the either-books-or-babies rule, having had three kids and written about twenty books, and thank God it wasn't the other way around. By the luck of race, class, money, and health, I could manage the double-tightrope trick—and especially by the support of my partner. He is not my wife; but he brought to marriage an assumption of mutual aid as its daily basis, and on that basis you can get a lot of work done. Our division of labor was fairly conventional; I was in charge of house, cooking, the kids, and novels, because I wanted to be, and he was in charge of being a professor, the car, the bills, and the garden, because he wanted to be. When the kids were babies I wrote at night; when they started school I wrote while they were at school; these days I write as a cow grazes. If I needed help he gave it without making it into a big favor, and—this is the central fact—he did not ever begrudge me the time I spent writing, or the blessing of my work.

That is the killer: the killing grudge, the envy, the jealousy, the spite that so often a man is allowed to hold, trained to hold, against anything a woman does that's not done in his service, for him, to feed his body, his comfort, his kids. A woman who tries to work against that grudge finds the blessing turned into a curse; she must rebel and go it alone, or fall silent in despair. Any artist must expect to work amid the total, rational indifference of everybody else to their work, for years, perhaps for life: but no artist can work well against daily, personal, vengeful resistance. And that's exactly what many women artists get from the people they love and live with.

I was spared all that. I was free—born free, lived free. And for years that personal freedom allowed me to ignore the degree to which my writing was controlled and constrained by judgments and assumptions which I thought were my own, but which were the internalized ideology of a male supremacist society. Even when subverting the conventions, I disguised my subversions from myself. It took me years to realize that I chose to work in such despised, marginal genres as science fiction, fantasy, young adult, precisely because they were excluded from critical, academic, canonical supervision, leaving the artist free; it took ten more years before I had the wits and guts to see and say that the exclusion of the genres from "literature" is unjustified, unjustifiable, and a matter not of quality but of politics. So too in my choice of subjects: until the mid-seventies I wrote my fiction about heroic adventures, high-tech futures, men in the halls of power, men—men were the central characters, the women were peripheral, secondary. Why don't you write about women? my mother asked me. I don't know how, I said. A stupid answer, but an honest one. I did not know how to write about women—very few of us did—because I thought that what men had written about women was the truth, was the true way to write about women. And I couldn't.

My mother could not give me what I needed. When feminism began to reawaken, she hated it, called it "those women's libbers"; but it was she who had steered me years and years before to what I would and did need, to Virginia Woolf. "We think back through our mothers," and we have many mothers, those of the body and those of the soul. What I needed was what feminism, feminist literary theory and criticism and practice, had to give me. And I can hold it in my hands—not only *Three Guineas*, my treasure in the days of poverty, but now all the wealth of *The Norton Anthology of Literature by Women* and the reprint houses and the women's presses. Our mothers have been returned to us. This time, let's hang on to them.

And it is feminism that has empowered me to criticize not only my society and myself but—for a moment now—feminism itself. The books-or-babies myth is not only a misogynist hang-up, it can be a feminist one. Some of the women I respect most, writing for publications that I depend on for my sense of women's solidarity and hope, continue to declare that it is "virtually impossible for a heterosexual woman to be a feminist," as if heterosexuality were heterosexism; and that social marginality, such as that of lesbian, childless, Black, or Native American women, "appears to be necessary" to form the feminist. Applying these judgments to myself, and believing that as a woman writing at this point I have to be a feminist to be worth beans, I find myself, once again, excluded—disappeared.

The rationale of the exclusionists, as I understand it, is that the material privilege and social approbation our society grants the heterosexual wife, and particularly the mother, prevent her solidarity with less privileged women and insulate her from the kind of anger and the kind of ideas that lead to feminist action. There is truth in this; maybe it's true for a lot of women; I can oppose it only with my experience, which is that feminism has been a life-saving *necessity* to women trapped in the wife/mother "role." What do the privilege and approbation accorded the housewife-mother by our society in fact consist of? Being the object of infinite advertising? Being charged by psychologists with total answerability for children's mental well-being, and by the government with total answerability for children's welfare, while being regularly equated with apple pie by sentimental warmongers? As a social "role," motherhood, for any woman I know, simply means that she does everything everybody else does plus bringing up the kids.

To push mothers back into "private life," a mythological space invented by the patriarchy, on the theory that their acceptance of the "role" of mother invalidates them for public, political, artistic responsibility, is to play Old Nobodaddy's game, by his rules, on his side.

In *Writing Beyond the Ending*, DuPlessis shows how women novelists write about the woman artist: they make her an ethical force, an activist trying "to change the life in which she is also immersed."[14] To have and bring up kids is to be about as immersed in life as one can be, but it does not always follow that one drowns. A lot of us can swim.

Again, whenever I give a version of this paper, somebody will pick up on this point and tell me that I'm supporting the Superwoman syndrome, saying that a woman *should* have kids write books be politically active and make perfect sushi. I am not saying that. We're all asked to be Superwoman; I'm not asking it, our society does that. All I can tell you is

14 DuPlessis, 101.

that I believe it's a lot easier to write books while bringing up kids than to bring up kids while working nine to five plus housekeeping. But that is what our society, while sentimentalizing over Mom and the Family, demands of most women—unless it refuses them any work at all and dumps them onto welfare and says, Bring up your kids on food stamps, Mom, we might want them for the army. Talk about superwomen, those are the superwomen. Those are the mothers up against the wall. Those are the marginal women, without either privacy or publicity; and it's because of them more than anyone else that the woman artist has a responsibility to "try to change the life in which she is also immersed."

And now I come back round to the bank of that lake, where the fisherwoman sits, our woman writer, who had to bring her imagination up short because it was getting too deeply immersed ... The imagination dries herself off, still swearing under her breath, and buttons up her blouse, and comes to sit beside the little girl, the fisherwoman's daughter. "Do you like books?" she says, and the child says, "Oh, yes. When I was a baby I used to eat them, but now I can read. I can read all of Beatrix Potter by myself, and when I grow up I'm going to write books, like Mama."

"Are you going to wait till your children grow up, like Jo March and Theodora?"

"Oh, I don't think so," says the child. "I'll just go ahead and do it."

"Then will you do as Harriet and Margaret and so many Harriets and Margarets have done and are still doing, and hassle through the prime of your life trying to do two full-time jobs that are incompatible with each other in practice, however enriching their interplay may be both to the life and the art?"

"I don't know," says the little girl. "Do I have to?"

"Yes," says the imagination, "if you aren't rich and you want kids."

"I might want one or two," says reason's child. "But why do women have two jobs where men only have one? It isn't reasonable, is it?"

"Don't ask me!" snaps the imagination. "I could think up a dozen better arrangements before breakfast! But who listens to me?"

The child sighs and watches her mother fishing. The fisherwoman, having forgotten that her line is no longer baited with the imagination, isn't catching anything, but she's enjoying the peaceful hour; and when the child speaks again she speaks softly. "Tell me, Auntie. What is the one thing a writer has to have?"

"I'll tell you," says the imagination. "The one thing a writer has to have is not balls. Nor is it a child-free space. Nor is it even, speaking strictly on the evidence, a room of her own, though that is an amazing help, as is the goodwill and cooperation of the opposite sex, or at least the local, in-house representative of it. But she doesn't have to have that. The one thing a writer has to have is a pencil and some paper. That's enough, so long as she knows that she and she alone is in charge of that pencil, and responsible, she and she alone, for what it writes on the paper. In other words, that she's free. Not wholly free. Never wholly free. Maybe very partially. Maybe only in this one act, this sitting for a snatched moment being a woman writing, fishing the mind's lake. But in this, responsible; in this, autonomous; in this, free."

"Auntie," says the little girl, "can I go fishing with you now?"

USES OF THE EROTIC: THE EROTIC AS POWER

Audre Lorde

THERE ARE MANY kinds of power, used and unused, acknowledged or otherwise. The erotic is a resource within each of us that lies in a deeply female and spiritual plane, firmly rooted in the power of our unexpressed or unrecognized feeling. In order to perpetuate itself, every oppression must corrupt or distort those various sources of power within the culture of the oppressed that can provide energy for change. For women, this has meant a suppression of the erotic as a considered source of power and information within our lives.

We have been taught to suspect this resource, vilified, abused, and devalued within western society. On the one hand, the superficially erotic has been encouraged as a sign of female inferiority; on the other hand, women have been made to suffer and to feel both contemptible and suspect by virtue of its existence.

It is a short step from there to the false belief that only by the suppression of the erotic within our lives and consciousness can women be truly strong. But that strength is illusory, for it is fashioned within the context of male models of power.

As women, we have come to distrust that power which rises from our deepest and nonrational knowledge. We have been warned against it all our lives by the male world, which values this depth of feeling enough to keep women around in order to exercise it in the service of men, but which fears this same depth too much to examine the possibilities of it within themselves. So women are maintained at a distant/inferior position to be psychically milked, much the same way ants maintain colonies of aphids to provide a life-giving substance for their masters.

But the erotic offers a well of replenishing and provocative force to the woman who does not fear its revelation, nor succumb to the belief that sensation is enough.

The erotic has often been misnamed by men and used against women. It has been made into the confused, the trivial, the psychotic, the plasticized sensation. For this reason, we have often turned away from the exploration and consideration of the erotic as a source of power and information, confusing it with its opposite, the pornographic. But pornography is a direct denial of the power of the erotic, for it represents the suppression of true feeling. Pornography emphasizes sensation without feeling.

The erotic is a measure between the beginnings of our sense of self and the chaos of our strongest feelings. It is an internal sense of satisfaction to which, once we have experienced it, we know we can aspire. For having experienced the fullness of this depth of feeling and recognizing its power, in honor and self-respect we can require no less of ourselves.

It is never easy to demand the most from ourselves, from our lives, from our work. To encourage excellence is to go beyond the encouraged mediocrity of our society is to encourage excellence. But giving in to the fear of feeling and working to capacity is a luxury only the unintentional can afford, and the unintentional are those who do not wish to guide their own destinies.

This internal requirement toward excellence which we learn from the erotic must not be misconstrued as demanding the impossible from ourselves nor from others. Such a demand incapacitates everyone in the process. For the erotic is not a question only of what we do; it is a question of how acutely and fully we can feel in the doing. Once we know the extent to which we are capable of feeling that sense of satisfaction and completion, we can then observe which of our various life endeavors bring us closest to that fullness. The aim of each thing which we do is to make our lives and the lives of our children richer and more possible. Within the celebration of the erotic in all our endeavors, my work becomes a conscious decision—a longed-for bed which I enter gratefully and from which I rise up empowered.

Of course, women so empowered are dangerous. So we are taught to separate the erotic demand from most vital areas of our lives other than sex. And the lack of concern for the erotic root and satisfactions of our work is felt in our disaffection from so much of what we do. For instance, how often do we truly love our work even at its most difficult?

The principal horror of any system which defines the good in terms of profit rather than in terms of human need, or which defines human need to the exclusion of the psychic and emotional components of that need—the principal horror of such a system is that it robs our work of its erotic value, its erotic power and life appeal and fulfillment. Such a system reduces work to a travesty of necessities, a duty by which we earn bread or oblivion for ourselves and those we love. But this is tantamount to blinding a painter and then telling her to improve her work, and to enjoy the act of painting. It is not only next to impossible, it is also profoundly cruel.

As women, we need to examine the ways in which our world can be truly different. I am speaking here of the necessity for reassessing the quality of all the aspects of our lives and of our work, and of how we move toward and through them.

The very word *erotic* comes from the Greek word *eros*, the personification of love in all its aspects—born of Chaos, and personifying creative power and harmony. When I speak of the erotic, then, I speak of it as an assertion of the lifeforce of women; of that creative energy empowered, the knowledge and use of which we are now reclaiming in our language, our history, our dancing, our loving, our work, our lives.

There are frequent attempts to equate pornography and eroticism, two diametrically opposed uses of the sexual. Because of these attempts, it has become fashionable to separate the spiritual (psychic and emotional) from the political, to see them as contradictory or antithetical. "What do you mean, a poetic revolutionary, a meditating gunrunner?" In the same way, we have attempted to separate the spiritual and the erotic, thereby reducing the spiritual to a world of flattened affect, a world of the ascetic who aspires to feel nothing. But nothing is farther from the truth. For the ascetic position is one of the highest fear, the gravest immobility. The severe abstinence of the ascetic becomes the ruling obsession. And it is one not of self discipline but of self-abnegation.

The dichotomy between the spiritual and the political is also false, resulting from an incomplete attention to our erotic knowledge. For the bridge which connects them is formed by the erotic—the sensual—those physical, emotional, and psychic expressions of what is deepest and strongest and richest within each of us, being shared: the passions of love, in its deepest meanings.

Beyond the superficial, the considered phrase, "It feels right to me," acknowledges the strength of the erotic into a true knowledge, for what that means is the first and most powerful guiding light toward any understanding. And understanding is a hand-maiden which can only wait upon, or clarify, that knowledge, deeply born. The erotic is the nurturer or nursemaid of all our deepest knowledge.

The erotic functions for me in several ways, and the first is in providing the power which comes from sharing deeply any pursuit with another person. The sharing of joy, whether physical, emotional, psychic, or intellectual, forms a bridge between the sharers which can be the basis for understanding much of what is not shared between them, and lessens the threat of their difference.

Another important way in which the erotic connection functions is the open and fearless underlining of my capacity for joy. In the way my body stretches to music and opens into response, hearkening to its deepest rhythms, so every level upon which I sense also opens to the erotically satisfying experience, whether it is dancing, building a bookcase, writing a poem, examining an idea.

That self-connection shared is a measure of the joy which I know myself to be capable of feeling, a reminder of my capacity for feeling. And that deep and irreplaceable knowledge of my capacity for joy comes to demand from all of my life that it be lived within the knowledge that such satisfaction is possible, and does not have to be called *marriage*, nor *god*, nor *an afterlife*.

This is one reason why the erotic is so feared, and so often relegated to the bedroom alone, when it is recognized at all. For once we begin to feel deeply all the aspects of our lives, we begin to demand from ourselves and from our life-pursuits that they feel in accordance with that joy which we know ourselves to be capable of. Our erotic knowledge empowers us, becomes a lens through which we scrutinize all aspects of our existence, forcing us to evaluate those aspects honestly in terms of their relative meaning within our lives. And this is a grave responsibility, projected from within each of us, not to settle for the convenient, the shoddy, the conventionally expected, nor the merely safe.

During World War II, we bought sealed plastic packets of white, uncolored margarine, with a tiny, intense pellet of yellow coloring perched like a topaz just inside the clear skin of the bag. We would leave the margarine out for a while to soften, and then we would pinch the little pellet to break it inside the bag, releasing the rich yellowness into the soft pale mass of margarine. Then taking it carefully between our fingers, we would knead it gently back and forth, over and over, until the color had spread throughout the whole pound bag of margarine, thoroughly coloring it. I find the erotic such a kernel within myself. When released from its intense and constrained pellet, it flows through and colors my life with a kind of energy that heightens and sensitizes and strengthens all my experience.

We have been raised to fear the yes within ourselves, our deepest cravings. But, once recognized, those which do not enhance our future lose their power and can be altered. The fear of our desires keeps them suspect and indiscriminately powerful, for to suppress any truth is to give it strength beyond endurance. The fear that we cannot grow beyond whatever distortions we may find within ourselves keeps us docile and loyal and obedient, externally defined, and leads us to accept many facets of our oppression as women.

When we live outside ourselves, and by that I mean on external directives only rather than from our internal knowledge and needs, when we live away from those erotic guides from within ourselves, then our lives are limited by external and alien forms, and we conform to the needs of a structure that is not based on human need, let alone an individual's. But when we begin to live from within outward, in touch with the power of the erotic within ourselves, and allowing that power to inform and illuminate our actions upon the world around us, then we begin to be responsible to ourselves in the deepest sense.

For as we begin to recognize our deepest feelings, we begin to give up, of necessity, being satisfied with suffering and self-negation, and with the numbness which so often seems like their only alternative in our society. Our acts against oppression become integral with self, motivated and empowered from within.

In touch with the erotic, I become less willing to accept powerlessness, or those other supplied states of being which are not native to me, such as resignation, despair, self-effacement, depression, self-denial.

And yes, there is a hierarchy. There is a difference between painting a back fence and writing a poem, but only one of quantity. And there is, for me, no difference between writing a good poem and moving into sunlight against the body of a woman I love.

This brings me to the last consideration of the erotic. To share the power of each other's feelings is different from using another's feelings as we would use a kleenex. When we look the other way from our experience, erotic or otherwise, we use rather than share the feelings of those others who participate in the experience with us. And use without consent of the used is abuse.

In order to be utilized, our erotic feelings must be recognized. The need for sharing deep feeling is a human need. But within the european-american tradition, this need is satisfied by certain proscribed erotic comings-together. These occasions are almost always characterized by a simultaneous looking away, a pretense of calling them something else, whether a religion, a fit, mob violence, or even playing doctor. And this misnaming of the need and the deed give rise to that distortion which results in pornography and obscenity—the abuse of feeling.

When we look away from the importance of the erotic in the development and sustenance of our power, or when we look away from ourselves as we satisfy our erotic needs in concert with others, we use each other as objects of satisfaction rather than share our joy in the satisfying, rather than make connection with our similarities and our differences. To refuse to be conscious of what we are feeling at any time, however comfortable that might seem, is to deny a large part of the experience, and to allow ourselves to be reduced to the pornographic, the abused, and the absurd.

The erotic cannot be felt secondhand. As a Black lesbian feminist, I have a particular feeling, knowledge, and understanding for those sisters with whom I have danced hard, played, or even fought. This deep participation has often been the forerunner for joint concerted actions not possible before.

But this erotic charge is not easily shared by women who continue to operate under an exclusively european-american male tradition. I know it was not available to me when I was trying to adapt my consciousness to this mode of living and sensation.

Only now, I find more and more women-identified women brave enough to risk sharing the erotic's electrical charge without having to look away, and without distorting the enormously powerful and creative nature of that exchange. Recognizing the power of the erotic within our lives can give us the energy to pursue genuine change within our world, rather than merely settling for a shift of characters in the same weary drama.

For not only do we touch our most profoundly creative source, but we do that which is female and self-affirming in the face of a racist, patriarchal, and anti-erotic society.

ANGER AND TENDERNESS

Adrienne Rich

> ... to understand is always an ascending movement; that is why comprehension ought always to be concrete, (one is never got out of the cave, one comes out of it.)
>
> Simone Weil, *First and Last Notebooks*

1

Entry from my journal, November 1960

My children cause me the most exquisite suffering of which I have any experience. It is the suffering of ambivalence: the murderous alternation between bitter resentment and raw-edged nerves, and blissful gratification and tenderness. Sometimes I seem to myself, in my feelings toward these tiny guiltless beings, a monster of selfishness and intolerance. Their voices wear away at my nerves, their constant needs, above all their need for simplicity and patience, fill me with despair at my own failures, despair too at my fate, which is to serve a function for which I was not fitted. And I am weak sometimes from held-in rage. There are times when I feel only death will free us from one another, when I envy the barren woman who has the luxury of her regrets but lives a life of privacy and freedom.[1]

And yet at other times I am melted with the sense of their helpless, charming and quite irresistible

1 The term "barren woman" was easy for me to use, unexamined, fifteen years ago. As should be clear throughout these pages, it seems to me now a term both tendentious and meaningless, based on a view of women which sees motherhood as our only positive definition.

beauty—their ability to go on loving and trusting—their staunchness and decency and unselfconsciousness. *I love them*. But it's in the enormity and inevitability of this love that the sufferings lie.

April 1962

A blissful love for my children engulfs me from time to time and seems almost to suffice—the aesthetic pleasure I have in these little, changing creatures, the sense of being loved, however dependently, the sense too that I'm not an utterly unnatural and shrewish mother—much though I am!

May 1965

To suffer with and for and against a child—maternally, egotistically, neurotically, sometimes with a sense of helplessness, sometimes with the illusion of learning wisdom—but always, everywhere, in body and soul, *with* that child—because that child is a piece of oneself.

To be caught up in waves of love and hate, jealousy even of the child's childhood; hope and fear for its maturity; longing to be free of responsibility, tied by every fiber of one's being.

That curious primitive reaction of protectiveness, the beast defending her cub, when anyone attacks or criticizes him—And yet no one more hard on him than I!

September 1965

Degradation of anger. Anger at a child. How shall I learn to absorb the violence and make explicit only the caring? Exhaustion of anger. Victory of will, too dearly bought—far too dearly!

March 1966

> Perhaps one is a monster—an anti-woman—something driven and without recourse to the normal and appealing consolations of love, motherhood, joy in others …

Unexamined assumptions: First, that a "natural" mother is a person without further identity, one who can find her chief gratification in being all day with small children, living at a pace tuned to theirs; that the isolation of mothers and children together in the home must be taken for granted; that maternal love is, and should be, quite literally selfless; that children and mothers are the "causes" of each others' suffering. I was haunted by the stereotype of the mother whose love is "unconditional"; and by the visual and literary images of motherhood as a single-minded identity. If I knew parts of myself existed that would never cohere to those images, weren't those parts then abnormal, monstrous? And—as my eldest son, now aged twenty-one, remarked on reading the above passages: "You seemed to feel you ought to love us all the time. But there *is* no human relationship where you love the other person at every moment." Yes, I tried to explain to him, but women—above all, mothers—have been supposed to love that way.

From the fifties and early sixties, I remember a cycle. It began when I had picked up a book or began trying to write a letter, or even found myself on the telephone with someone toward whom my voice betrayed eagerness, a rush of sympathetic energy. The child (or children) might be absorbed in busyness, in his own dreamworld; but as soon as he felt me gliding into a world which did not include him, he would come to pull at my hand, ask for help, punch at the typewriter keys. And I would feel his wants at such a moment as fraudulent, as an attempt moreover to defraud me of living even for fifteen minutes as myself. My anger would rise; I would feel the futility of any attempt to salvage myself, and also the inequality between us: my needs always balanced against those of a child, and always losing. I could love so much better, I told myself, after even a quarter-hour of selfishness, of peace, of detachment from my children. A few minutes! But it was as if an invisible thread would pull taut between us and break, to the child's sense of inconsolable abandonment, if I moved—not even physically, but in spirit—into a realm beyond our tightly circumscribed life together. It was as if my placenta had begun to refuse him oxygen. Like so many women, I waited with impatience for the moment when their father would return from work, when for an hour or two at least the circle drawn around mother and children would grow looser, the intensity between us slacken, because there was another adult in the house.

I did not understand that this circle, this magnetic field in which we lived, was not a natural phenomenon. Intellectually, I must have known it. But the emotion-charged, tradition-heavy form in which I found myself cast as the Mother seemed, then, as ineluctable as the tides. And, because of this form—this microcosm in which my children and I formed a tiny, private emotional cluster, and in which (in bad weather or when someone was ill) we sometimes passed days at a time without seeing another adult except for their father—there *was* authentic need underlying my child's invented claims upon me when I seemed to be wandering away from him. He was reassuring himself that warmth, tenderness, continuity, solidity were still there for him, in my person. My singularity, my uniqueness in the world as his mother—perhaps more dimly also as Woman—evoked a need vaster than any single human being could satisfy, except by loving continuously, unconditionally, from dawn to dark, and often in the middle of the night.

2

In a living room in 1975, I spent an evening with a group of women poets, some of whom had children. One had brought hers along, and they slept or played in adjoining rooms. We talked of poetry, and also of infanticide, of the case of a local woman, the mother of eight, who had been in severe depression since the birth of her third child, and who had recently murdered and decapitated her two youngest, on her suburban front lawn. Several women in the group, feeling a direct connection with her desperation, had signed a letter to the local newspaper protesting the way her act was perceived by the press and handled by the community mental health system. Every woman in that room who had children, every poet, could identify with her. We spoke of the wells of anger that her story cleft open in us. We spoke of our own moments of murderous anger at our children, because there was no one and nothing else on which to discharge anger. We spoke in the sometimes tentative, sometimes rising, sometimes bitterly witty, unrhetorical tones and language of women who had met together over our common work, poetry, and who found another common ground in an unacceptable, but undeniable anger. The words are being spoken now, are being written down; the taboos are being broken, the masks of motherhood are cracking through.

For centuries no one talked of these feelings. I became a mother in the family-centered, consumer-oriented, Freudian-American world of the 1950s. My husband spoke eagerly of the children we would have; my parents-in-law awaited the birth of their grandchild. I had no idea of what I wanted, what I could or could not choose. I only knew that to have a child was to assume adult womanhood to the full, to prove myself, to be “like other women.”

To be “like other women” had been a problem for

me. From the age of thirteen or fourteen, I had felt I was only acting the part of a feminine creature. At the age of sixteen my fingers were almost constantly ink-stained. The lipstick and high heels of the era were difficult-to-manage disguises. In 1945 I was writing poetry seriously, and had a fantasy of going to postwar Europe as a journalist, sleeping among the ruins in bombed cities, recording the rebirth of civilization after the fall of the Nazis. But also, like every other girl I knew, I spent hours trying to apply lipstick more adroitly, straightening the wandering seams of stockings, talking about "boys." There were two different compartments, already, to my life. But writing poetry, and my fantasies of travel and self-sufficiency, seemed more real to me; I felt that as an incipient "real woman" I was a fake. Particularly was I paralyzed when I encountered young children. I think I felt men could be—wished to be—conned into thinking I was truly "feminine"; a child, I suspected, could see through me like a shot. This sense of acting a part created a curious sense of guilt, even though it was a part demanded for survival.

I have a very clear, keen memory of myself the day after I was married: I was sweeping a floor. Probably the floor did not really need to be swept; probably I simply did not know what else to do with myself. But as I swept that floor I thought: "Now I am a woman. This is an age-old action, this is what women have always done." I felt I was bending to some ancient form, too ancient to question. *This is what women have always done.*

As soon as I was visibly and clearly pregnant, I felt, for the first time in my adolescent and adult life, not-guilty. The atmosphere of approval in which I was bathed—even by strangers on the street, it seemed—was like an aura I carried with me, in which doubts, fears, misgivings, met with absolute denial. *This is what women have always done.* Two days before my first son was born, I broke out in a rash which was tentatively diagnosed as measles, and was admitted to a hospital for contagious diseases to await the onset of labor. I felt for the first time a great deal of conscious fear, and guilt toward my unborn child, for having "failed" him with my body in this way. In rooms near mine were patients with polio; no one was allowed to enter my room except in a hospital gown and mask. If during pregnancy I had felt in any vague command of my situation, I felt now totally dependent on my obstetrician, a huge, vigorous, paternal man, abounding with optimism and assurance, and given to pinching my cheek. I had gone through a healthy pregnancy, but as if tranquilized or sleep-walking. I had taken a sewing class in which I produced an unsightly and ill-cut maternity jacket which I never wore; I had made curtains for the baby's room, collected baby clothes, blotted

out as much as possible the woman I had been a few months earlier. My second book of poems was in press, but I had stopped writing poetry, and read little except household magazines and books on child-care. I felt myself perceived by the world simply as a pregnant woman, and it seemed easier, less disturbing, to perceive myself so. After my child was born the "measles" were diagnosed as an allergic reaction to pregnancy.

Within two years, I was pregnant again, and writing in a notebook:

November 1956

Whether it's the extreme lassitude of early pregnancy or something more fundamental, I don't know; but of late I've felt, toward poetry,—both reading and writing it—nothing but boredom and indifference. Especially toward my own and that of my immediate contemporaries. When I receive a letter soliciting mss., or someone alludes to my "career," I have a strong sense of wanting to deny all responsibility for and interest in that person who writes—or who wrote.

If there is going to be a real break in my writing life, this is as good a time for it as any. I have been dissatisfied with myself, my work, for a long time.

My husband was a sensitive, affectionate man who wanted children and who—unusual in the professional, academic world of the fifties—was willing to "help." But it was clearly understood that this "help" was an act of generosity; that *his* work, *his* professional life, was the real work in the family; in fact, this was for years not even an issue between us. I understood that my struggles as a writer were a kind of luxury, a peculiarity of mine; my work brought in almost no money: it even cost money, when I hired a household helper to allow me a few hours a week to write. "Whatever I ask he tries to give me," I wrote in March 1958, "but always the initiative has to be mine." I experienced my depressions, bursts of anger, sense of entrapment, as burdens my husband was forced to bear because he loved me; I felt grateful to be loved in spite of bringing him those burdens.

But I was struggling to bring my life into focus. I had never really given up on poetry, nor on gaining some control over my existence. The life of a Cambridge tenement backyard swarming with children, the repetitious cycles of laundry, the night-wakings, the interrupted moments of peace or of engagement with ideas, the ludicrous dinner parties at which young wives, some with advanced degrees, all seriously and intelligently dedicated to their children's welfare and their husbands' careers, attempted to reproduce the amenities of Brahmin Boston, amid French recipes and the pretense of effortlessness—above all, the ultimate lack of seriousness with which women were regarded in that world—all of this defied analysis at that time, but I *knew* I had to remake my own life. I did not then understand that we—the women of that academic community—as in so many middle-class communities of the period—were expected to fill both the part of the Victorian Lady of Leisure, the Angel in the House, and also of the Victorian cook, scullery maid, laundress, governess, and nurse. I only sensed that there were false distractions sucking at me, and I wanted desperately to strip my life down to what was essential.

June 1958

These months I've been all a tangle of irritations deepening to anger: bitterness, disillusion with society and with myself; beating out at the world, rejecting out of hand. What, if anything, has been positive? Perhaps the attempt to remake my life, to save it from mere drift and the passage of time …

The work that is before me is serious and difficult and not at all clear even as to plan. Discipline of mind and spirit, uniqueness of expression, ordering of daily existence, the most effective functioning of the human self—these are the chief things I wish to achieve. So far the only beginning I've been able to make is to waste less time. That is what some of the rejection has been all about.

By July of 1958 I was again pregnant. The new life of my third—and, as I determined, my last—child, was a kind of turning for me. I had learned that my body was not under my control; I had not intended to bear a third child. I knew now better than I had ever known what another pregnancy, another new infant, meant for my body and spirit. Yet, I did not think of having an abortion. In a sense, my third son was more actively chosen than either of his brothers; by the time I knew

I was pregnant with him, I was not sleepwalking anymore.

August 1958 (Vermont)

I write this as the early rays of the sun light up our hillside and eastern windows. Rose with [the baby] at 5:30 A.M. and have fed him and breakfasted. This is one of the few mornings on which I haven't felt terrible mental depression and physical exhaustion.

... I have to acknowledge to myself that I would not have chosen to have more children, that I was beginning to look to a time, not too far off, when I should again be free, no longer so physically tired, pursuing a more or less intellectual and creative life ... The *only* way I can develop now is through much harder, more continuous, connected work than my present life makes possible. Another child means postponing this for some years longer—and years at my age are significant, not to be tossed lightly away.

And yet, somehow, something, call it Nature or that affirming fatalism of the human creature, makes me aware of the inevitable as already part of me, not to be contended against so much as brought to bear as an additional weapon against drift, stagnation and spiritual death. (For it is really death that I have been fearing—the crumbling to death of that scarcely-bom physiognomy which my whole life has been a battle to give birth to—a recognizable, autonomous self, a creation in poetry and in life.)

If more effort has to be made then I will make it. If more despair has to be lived through, I think I can anticipate it correctly and live through it.

Meanwhile, in a curious and unanticipated way, we really do welcome the birth of our child.

There was, of course, an economic as well as a spiritual margin which allowed me to think of a third child's birth not as my own death-warrant but as an "additional weapon against death." My body, despite recurrent flares of arthritis, was a healthy one; I had good prenatal care; we were not living on the edge of malnutrition; I knew that all my children would be fed, clothed, breathe fresh air; in fact it did not occur to me that it could be otherwise. But, in another sense, beyond that physical margin, I knew I was fighting for my life through, against, and with the lives of my children, though very little else was clear to me. I had been trying to give birth to myself; and in some grim, dim way I was determined to use even pregnancy and parturition in that process.

Before my third child was bom I decided to have no more children, to be sterilized, (Nothing is removed from a woman's body during this operation; ovulation and menstruation continue. Yet the language suggests a cutting- or burning-away of her essential womanhood, just as the old word "barren" suggests a woman eternally empty and lacking.) My husband, although he supported my decision, asked whether I was sure it would not leave me feeling "less feminine." In order to have the operation at all, I had to present a letter, counter-signed by my husband, assuring the committee of physicians who approved such operations that I had already produced three children, and stating my reasons for having no more. Since I had had rheumatoid arthritis for some years, I could give a reason acceptable to the male panel who sat on my case; my own judgment would not have been acceptable. When I awoke from the operation, twenty-four hours after my child's birth, a young nurse looked at my chart and remarked coldly: "Had yourself spayed, did you?"

The first great birth-control crusader, Margaret Sanger, remarks that of the hundreds of women who wrote to her pleading for contraceptive information in the early part of the twentieth century, all spoke of wanting the health and strength to be better mothers to the children they already had; or of wanting to be physically affectionate to their husbands without dread of conceiving. None was refusing motherhood altogether, or asking for an easy life. These women—mostly poor, many still in their teens, all with several children—simply felt they could no longer do "right" by their families, whom they expected to go on serving and rearing. Yet there always has been, and there remains, intense fear of the suggestion that women shall have the final say as to how our bodies are to be used. It is as if the suffering of the mother, the primary identification of woman *as* the mother—were so necessary to the emotional grounding of human society that the mitigation, or removal, of that suffering, that identification, must be fought at every level, including the level of refusing to question it at all.

3

"Vous travaillez pour l'armée, madame?" (You are working for the army?), a Frenchwoman said to me early in the Vietnam war, on hearing I had three sons.

April 1965

Anger, weariness, demoralization. Sudden bouts of weeping. A sense of insufficiency to the moment and to eternity …

Paralyzed by the sense that there exists a mesh of relations, between e.g. my rejection and anger at [my eldest child], my sensual life, pacifism, sex (I mean in its broadest significance, not merely physical desire)—an interconnectedness which, if I could see it, make it valid, would give me back myself, make it possible to function lucidly and passionately—Yet I grope in and out among these

dark webs—
I weep, and weep, and the sense of powerlessness spreads like a cancer through my being.

August 1965, 3:30 A.M.
Necessity for a more unyielding discipline of my life.
Recognize the uselessness of blind anger.
Limit society.
Use children's school hours better, for work & solitude.
Refuse to be distracted from own style of life.
Less waste.
Be harder & harder on poems.

Once in a while someone used to ask me, "Don't you ever write poems about your children?" The male poets of my generation did write poems about their children—especially their daughters. For me, poetry was where I lived as no-one's mother, where I existed as myself.

The bad and the good moments are inseparable for me. I recall the times when, suckling each of my children, I saw his eyes open full to mine, and realized each of us was fastened to the other, not only by mouth and breast, but through our mutual gaze: the depth, calm, passion, of that dark blue, maturely focused look. I recall the physical pleasure of having my full breast suckled at a time when I had no other physical pleasure in the world except the guilt-ridden pleasure of addictive eating. I remember early the sense of conflict, of a battleground none of us had chosen, of being an observer who, like it or not, was also an actor in an endless contest of wills. This was what it meant to me to have three children under the age of seven. But I recall too each child's individual body, his slenderness, wiriness, softness, grace, the beauty of little boys who have not been taught that the male body must be rigid. I remember moments of peace when for some reason it was possible to go to the bathroom alone. I remember being uprooted from already meager sleep to answer a childish nightmare, pull up a blanket, warm a consoling bottle, lead a half-asleep child to the toilet. I remember going back to bed starkly awake, brittle with anger, knowing that my broken sleep would make next day a hell, that there would be more nightmares, more need for consolation, because out of my weariness I would rage at those children for no reason they could understand. I remember thinking I would never dream again (the unconscious of the young mother—where does it entrust its messages, when dream-sleep is denied her for years?)

For many years I shrank from looking back on the first decade of my children's lives. In snapshots of the period I see a smiling young woman, in maternity clothes or bent over a half-naked baby; gradually she stops smiling, wears a distant, half-melancholy look, as if she were listening for something. In time my sons grew older, I began changing my own life, we began to talk to each other as equals. Together we lived through my leaving the marriage, and through their father's suicide. We became survivors, four distinct people with strong bonds connecting us. Because I always tried to tell them the truth, because their every new independence meant new freedom for me, because we trusted each other even when we wanted different things, they became, at a fairly young age, self-reliant and open to the unfamiliar. Something told me that if they had survived my angers, my self-reproaches, and still trusted my love and each others', they were strong. Their lives have not been, will not be, easy; but their very existences seem a gift to me, their vitality, humor, intelligence, gentleness, love of life, their separate life-currents which here and there stream into my own. I don't know how we made it from their embattled childhood and my embattled motherhood into a mutual recognition of ourselves and each other. Probably that mutual recognition, over-laid by social and traditional circumstance, was always there, from the first gaze between the mother and the infant at the breast. But I do know that for years I believed I should never have been anyone's mother, that because I felt my own needs acutely and often expressed them violently, I was Kali, Medea, the sow that devours her farrow, the unwomanly woman in flight from womanhood, a Nietzschean monster. Even today, rereading old journals, remembering, I feel grief and anger; but their objects are no longer myself and my children. I feel grief at the waste of myself in those years, anger at the mutilation and manipulation of the relationship between mother and child, which is the great original source and experience of love.

On an early spring day in the 1970s, I meet a young woman friend on the street. She has a tiny infant against her breast, in a bright cotton sling; its face is pressed against her blouse, its tiny hand clutches a piece of the cloth. "How old is she?" I ask. "Just two weeks old," the mother tells me. I am amazed to feel in myself a passionate longing to have, once again, such a small, new being clasped against my body. The baby belongs there, curled, suspended asleep between her mother's breasts, as she belonged curled in the womb. The young mother—who already has a three-year-old—speaks of how quickly one forgets the pure pleasure of having this new creature, immaculate, perfect. And I walk away from her drenched with memory, with envy. Yet I know other things: that her life is far from simple; she is a mathematician who now has two children under the age of four; she is living even now in the rhythms of other lives—not only the regular cry of the infant but her three-year-old's needs, her husband's problems.

In the building where I live, women are still raising children alone, living day in and day out within their individual family units, doing the laundry, herding the tricycles to the park, waiting for the husbands to come home. There is a baby-sitting pool and a children's playroom, young fathers push prams on weekends, but child-care is still the individual responsibility of the individual woman. I envy the sensuality of having an infant of two weeks curled against one's breast; I do not envy the turmoil of the elevator full of small children, babies howling in the laundromat, the apartment in winter where pent-up seven- and eight-year-olds have one adult to look to for their frustrations, reassurances, the grounding of their lives.

4

But, it will be said, this is the human condition, this interpenetration of pain and pleasure, frustration and fulfillment. I might have told myself the same thing, fifteen or eighteen years ago. But the patriarchal institution of motherhood is not the "human condition" any more than rape, prostitution, and slavery are. (Those who speak largely of the human condition are usually those most exempt from its oppressions—whether of sex, race, or servitude.)

Motherhood—unmentioned in the histories of conquest and serfdom, wars and treaties, exploration and imperialism—has a history, it has an ideology, it is more fundamental than tribalism or nationalism. My individual, seemingly private pains as a mother, the individual, seemingly private pains of the mothers around me and before me, whatever our class or color, the regulation of women's reproductive power by men in every totalitarian system and every socialist revolution, the legal and technical control by men of contraception, fertility, abortion, obstetrics, gynecology, and extrauterine reproductive experiments—all are essential to the patriarchal system, as is the negative or suspect status of women who are not mothers.

Throughout patriarchal mythology, dream-symbolism, theology, language, two ideas flow side by side: one, that the female body is impure, corrupt, the site of discharges, bleedings, dangerous to masculinity, a source of moral and physical contamination, "the devil's gateway." On the other hand, as mother the woman is beneficent, sacred, pure, asexual, nourishing; and the physical potential for motherhood—that same body with its bleedings and mysteries—is her single destiny and justification in life. These two ideas have become deeply internalized in women, even in the most independent of us, those who seem to lead the freest lives.

In order to maintain two such notions, each in its contradictory purity, the masculine imagination has had to divide women, to see us, and force us to see ourselves, as polarized into good or evil, fertile or barren, pure or impure. The asexual Victorian angel-wife and the Victorian prostitute were institutions created by this double thinking, which had nothing to do with women's actual sensuality and everything to do with the male's subjective experience of women. The political and economic expediency of this kind of thinking is most unashamedly and dramatically to be found where sexism and racism become one. The social historian A. W. Calhoun describes the encouragement of the rape of Black women by the sons of white planters, in a deliberate effort to produce more mulatto slaves, mulattos being considered more valuable. He quotes two mid-nineteenth-century southern writers on the subject of women:

> "The heaviest part of the white racial burden in slavery was the African woman of strong sex instincts and devoid of a sexual conscience, at the

> white man's door, in the white man's dwelling." … "Under the institution of slavery, the attack against the integrity of white civilization was made by the insidious influence of the lascivious hybrid woman at the point of weakest resistance. In the uncompromising purity of the white mother and wife of the upper classes lay the one assurance of the future purity of the race."[2]

The motherhood created by rape is not only degraded; the raped woman is turned into the criminal, the *attacker*. But who brought the Black woman to the white man's door, whose absence of a sexual conscience produced the financially profitable mulatto children? Is it asked whether the "pure" white mother and wife was not also raped by the white planter, since she was assumed to be devoid of "strong sexual instinct?" In the American South, as elsewhere, it was economically necessary that children be produced; the mothers, Black and white, were a means to this end.

Neither the "pure" nor the "lascivious" woman, neither the so-called mistress nor the slave woman, neither the woman praised for reducing herself to a brood animal nor the woman scorned and penalized as an "old maid" or a "dyke," has had any real autonomy or selfhood to gain from this subversion of the female body (and hence of the female mind). Yet, because short-term advantages are often the only ones visible to the powerless, we, too, have played our parts in continuing this subversion.

2 Arthur W. Calhoun, *A Social History of the American Family from Colonial Times to the Present* (Norman, OK: Arthur H. Clark Company, 1917). See also Gerda Lerner, *Black Women in White America: A Documentary History* (New York: Vintage, 1973), 149–50.

5

Most of the literature of infant care and psychology has assumed that the process toward individuation is essentially the *child's* drama, played out against and with a parent or parents who are, for better or worse, givens. Nothing could have prepared me for the realization that I *was* a mother, one of those givens, when I knew I was still in a state of uncreation myself. That calm, sure, unambivalent woman who moved through the pages of the manuals I read seemed as unlike me as an astronaut. Nothing, to be sure, had prepared me for the intensity of relationship already existing between me and a creature I had carried in my body and now held in my arms and fed from my breasts. Throughout pregnancy and nursing, women are urged to relax, to mime the serenity of madonnas. No one mentions the psychic crisis of bearing a first child, the excitation of long-buried feelings about one's own mother, the sense of confused power and powerlessness, of being taken over on the one hand and of touching new physical and psychic potentialities on the other, a heightened sensibility which can be exhilarating, bewildering, and exhausting. No one mentions the strangeness of attraction—which can be as single-minded and overwhelming as the early days of a love affair—to a being so tiny, so dependent, so folded-in to itself—who is, and yet is not, part of oneself.

From the beginning the mother caring for her child is involved in a continually changing dialogue, crystallized in such moments as when, hearing her child's cry, she feels milk rush into her breasts; when, as the child first suckles, the uterus begins contracting and returning to its normal size, and when later, the child's mouth, caressing the nipple, creates waves of sensuality in the womb where it once lay; or when, smelling the breast even in sleep, the child starts to root and grope for the nipple.

The child gains her first sense of her own existence from the mother's responsive gestures and expressions. It's as if, in the mother's eyes, her smile, her stroking touch, the child first reads the message: *You are there!* And the mother, too, is discovering her own existence newly. She is connected with this other being, by the most mundane and the most invisible strands, in a way she can be connected with no one else except in the deep past of her infant connection with her own mother. And she, too, needs to struggle from that one-to-one intensity into new realization, or reaffirmation, of her being-unto-herself.

The act of suckling a child, like a sexual act, may be tense, physically painful, charged with cultural feelings of inadequacy and guilt; or, like a sexual act, it can be a physically delicious, elementally soothing experience, filled with a tender sensuality.

But just as lovers have to break apart after sex and become separate individuals again, so the mother has to wean herself from the infant and the infant from herself. In psychologies of child-rearing the emphasis is placed on "letting the child go" for the child's sake. But the mother needs to let it go as much or more for her own.

Motherhood, in the sense of an intense, reciprocal relationship with a particular child, or children, is *one part* of female process; it is not an identity for all time. The housewife in her mid-Forties may jokingly say, "I feel like someone out of a job." But in the eyes of society, once having been mothers, what are we, if not always mothers? The process of "letting-go"—though we are charged with blame if we do not—is an act of revolt against the grain of patriarchal culture. But it is not enough to let our children go; we need selves of our own to return to.

To have borne and reared a child is to have done that thing which patriarchy joins with physiology to render into the definition of femaleness. But also, it can mean the experiencing of one's own body and emotions in a powerful way. We experience not only physical, fleshly changes but the feeling of a change in character. We learn, often through painful self-discipline and self-cauterization, those qualities which are supposed to be "innate" in us: patience, self-sacrifice, the willingness to repeat endlessly the small, routine chores of socializing a human being. We are also, often to our amazement, flooded with feelings both of love and violence intenser and fiercer than any we had ever known. (A well-known pacifist, also a mother, said recently on a platform: "If anyone laid a hand on *my* child, I'd murder him.")

These and similar experiences are not easily put aside. Small wonder that women gritting their teeth at the incessant demands of child-care still find it hard to acknowledge their children's growing independence of them; still feel they must be at home, on the *qui vive*, be that ear always tuned for the sound of emergency, of being needed. Children grow up, not in a smooth ascending curve, but jaggedly, their needs inconstant as weather. Cultural "norms" are marvelously powerless to decide, in a child of eight or ten, what gender s/he will assume on a given day, or how s/he will meet emergency, loneliness, pain, hunger. One is constantly made aware that a human existence is anything but linear, long before the labyrinth of puberty; because a human being of six is still a human being.

In a tribal or even a feudal culture a child of six would have serious obligations; ours have none. But also, the woman at home with children is not believed to be doing serious work; she is just supposed to be acting out of maternal instinct, doing chores a man would never take on, largely uncritical of the meaning of what she does. So child and mother alike are depreciated, because only grown men and women in the paid labor force are supposed to be "productive."

The power-relations between mother and child are often simply a reflection of power-relations in patriarchal society: "You will do this because I know what is good for you" is difficult to distinguish from "You will do this because I can *make* you." Powerless women have always used mothering as a channel—narrow but deep—for their own human will to power, their need to return upon the world what it has visited on them. The child dragged by the arm across the room to be washed, the child cajoled, bullied, and bribed into taking "one more bite" of a detested food, is more than just a child which must be reared according to cultural traditions of "good mothering." S/he is a piece of reality, of the world, which can be acted on, even modified, by a woman restricted from acting on anything else except inert materials like dust and food.[3]

3 1986: the work of the Swiss psychotherapist Alice Miller has made me reflect further on the material in this chapter and in Chapters IX and X. Miller identifies the "hidden cruelty" in child-rearing as the repetition of "poisonous pedagogy" inflicted by the parents of the generation before and as providing the soil in which obedience to authoritarianism and fascism take root. She notes that "there is one taboo that has withstood all the recent efforts at demystification: the idealization of mother love" (*The Drama of the Gifted Child: How Narcissistic Parents Form and Deform the Emotional Lives of Their Talented Children* [New York: Harper & Row, 1981], 4). Her work traces the damages of that idealization (of both parents, but especially the mother) upon children forbidden to name or protest their suffering, who side with their parents against themselves. Miller notes, "I cannot listen to my child with empathy if I am inwardly preoccupied with being a good mother; I cannot be open to what she is telling me" (*For Your Own Good: Hidden Cruelty in Child-rearing and the Roots of Violence* [New York: Farrar, Straus & Giroux, 1985], 258). Miller explores the sources of what has been defined as *child abuse*—i.e., physical violation and sadistic punishment—but she is equally concerned with the "gentle violence" of child-rearing, including that of "antiauthoritarian" or "alternative" prescriptions, based on the denial and suppression of the child's own vitality and feelings.

6

When I try to return to the body of the young woman of twenty-six, pregnant for the first time, who fled from the physical knowledge of her pregnancy and at the same time from her intellect and vocation, I realize that I was effectively alienated from my real body and my real spirit by the institution—not the fact—of motherhood. This institution—the foundation of human society as we know it—allowed me only certain views, certain expectations, whether embodied in the booklet in my obstetrician's waiting room, the novels I had read, my mother-in-law's approval, my memories of my own mother, the Sistine Madonna or she of the Michelangelo *Pietà*, the floating notion that a woman pregnant is a woman calm in her fulfillment or, simply, a woman waiting. Women have always been seen as waiting: waiting to be asked, waiting for our menses, in fear lest they do or do not come, waiting for men to come home from wars, or from work, waiting for children to grow up, or for the birth of a new child, or for menopause.

In my own pregnancy I dealt with this waiting, this female fate, by denying every active, powerful aspect of myself. I became dissociated both from my immediate, present, bodily experience and from my reading, thinking, writing life. Like a traveler in an airport where her plane is several hours delayed, who leafs through magazines she would never

Miller does not consider the predominance of women as primary caregivers, the investment of authoritarian or fascist systems in perpetuating male control of women's sexuality and reproductivity, or the structural *differences* between father-as-parent and mother-as-parent. She does acknowledge that in America, women especially "have discovered the power of their knowledge. They do not shrink from pointing out the poisonous nature of false information, even though it has been well-concealed for millennia behind sacrosanct and well-meaning labels" (*For Your Own Good*, p. xii).

ordinarily read, surveys shops whose contents do not interest her, I committed myself to an outward serenity and a profound inner boredom. If boredom is simply a mask for anxiety, then I had learned, as a woman, to be supremely bored rather than to examine the anxiety underlying my Sistine tranquility. My body, finally truthful, paid me back in the end: I was allergic to pregnancy.

I have come to believe that female biology—the diffuse, intense sensuality radiating out from clitoris, breasts, uterus, vagina; the lunar cycles of menstruation; the gestation and fruition of life which can take place in the female body—has far more radical implications than we have yet come to appreciate. Patriarchal thought has limited female biology to its own narrow specifications. The feminist vision has recoiled from female biology for these reasons; it will, I believe, come to view our physicality as a resource, rather than a destiny. In order to live a fully human life we require not only *control* of our bodies (though control is a prerequisite); we must touch the unity and resonance of our physicality, our bond with the natural order, the corporeal ground of our intelligence.

The ancient, continuing envy, awe, and dread of the male for the female capacity to create life has repeatedly taken the form of hatred for every other female aspect of creativity. Not only have women been told to stick to motherhood, but we have been told that our intellectual or aesthetic creations were inappropriate, inconsequential, or scandalous, an attempt to become "like men," or to escape from the "real" tasks of adult womanhood: marriage and childbearing. To "think like a man" has been both praise and prison for women trying to escape the body-trap. No wonder that many intellectual and creative women have insisted that they were "human beings" first and women only incidentally, have minimized their physicality and their bonds with other women. The body has been made so problematic for women that it has often seemed easier to shrug it off and travel as a disembodied spirit.

But this reaction against the body is now coming into synthesis with new inquiries into the actual—as opposed to the culturally warped—power inherent in female biology, however we choose to use it, and by no means limited to the maternal function.

My own story, which is woven throughout this book, is only one story. What I carried away in the end was a determination to heal—insofar as an individual woman can, and as much as possible with other women—the separation between mind and body; never again to lose myself both psychically and physically in that way. Slowly I came to understand the paradox contained in "my" experience of motherhood; that, although different from many other women's experiences it was not unique; and that only in shedding the illusion of my uniqueness could I hope, as a woman, to have any authentic life at all.

AN INTERVIEW WITH AUDRE LORDE

Audre Lorde and Adrienne Rich

ADRIENNE RICH:
What do you mean when you say that those two essays—"Poems Are Not Luxuries" and "Uses of the Erotic"—are really progressions?[1,2]

AUDRE LORDE:
They're part of something that's not finished yet. I don't know what the rest of it is, but they're very clear progressions to me, in feeling out something that is connected also with the first piece of prose I ever wrote. The one thread I feel coming through over and over in my life is the battle to preserve my perceptions, the battle to win through and to keep them—pleasant or unpleasant, painful or whatever—

AR: And however much they were denied.

AL: And however much they were denied. And however painful some of them were. When I think of the way in which I courted punishment, the way in which I just swam into it: "If this is the only way you're going to deal with me, you're gonna have to deal with me this way."

AR: You're talking about as a young child?

1 Audre Lorde, "Poems Are Not Luxuries," in *Chrysalis: A Magazine of Female Culture*, no. 3 (1977), 7–9.
2 Audre Lorde, "Uses of the Erotic: The Erotic as Power" (paper delivered at the Fourth Berkshire Conference on the History of Women, Mount Holyoke College, August 25, 1978), in this volume, p. 169.

AL: I'm talking about as an infant, as a very young child, over and over again throughout my life. I kept myself through feeling. I lived through it. And at such a subterranean level, I think, that I didn't know *how* to talk. I was really busy feeling out other ways of getting and giving information and whatever else I could, because talking wasn't where it was at. People were talking all around me all the time—and not either getting or giving much that was useful to them or to me, or that made sense to me at the time.

AR: And not listening to what you tried to say, if you did speak.

AL: When you asked how I began writing, I told you how poetry functioned specifically for me from the time I was very young, from nursery rhymes. When someone said to me, "How do you feel?" or "What do you think?" or asked another direct question, I would recite a poem, and somewhere in that poem would be the feeling, somewhere in it would be the piece of information. It might be a line. It might be an image. The poem was my response.

AR: Like a translation into this poem that already existed, of something you knew in a preverbal way. So the poem became your language?

AL: Yes. I remember reading in the children's room of the library, I couldn't have been past the second or third grade, but I remember the book. It was illustrated by Arthur Rackham, a book of poems. These were old books, the library in Harlem used to get the oldest books, in the worst condition. Walter de la Mare's "The Listeners"—I will never forget that poem.

AR: Where the traveler rides up to the door of the empty house?

AL: That's right. He knocks at the door and nobody answers. "'Is there anybody there?' he said." That poem imprinted itself on me. And finally, he's beating down the door and nobody answers, and he has a feeling that there really is somebody in there. And then he turns his horse and he says, "'Tell them I came, and nobody answered. That I kept my word,' he said." I used to recite that poem to myself all the time. It was one of my favorites. And if you'd asked me, what is it about, I don't think I could have told you. But this was the first cause of my own writing, my need to say things I couldn't say otherwise, when I couldn't find other poems to serve.

AR: You had to make your own.

AL: There were so many complex emotions, it seemed, for which poems did not exist. I had to find a secret way to express my feelings. I used to memorize my poems. I would say them out, I didn't use to write them down. I had this long fund of poetry in my head. And I remember trying when I was in high school not to think in poems. I saw the way other people thought, and it was an amazement to me—step by step, not in bubbles up from chaos that you had to anchor with words ... I really do believe I learned this from my mother.

AR: Learned what from your mother?

AL: The important value of nonverbal communication, beneath language. My life depended on it. At the same time living in the world and using language. And I didn't want to have anything to do with the way she was using language. My mother had a strange way with words; if one didn't serve her or wasn't strong enough, she'd just make up another word, and then that word would enter our family language forever, and woe betide any of us who forgot it. But I think I got another message from her … that there was a whole powerful world of nonverbal communication and contact between people that was absolutely essential and that was what you had to learn to decipher and use. One of the reasons I had so much trouble growing up was that my parents, my mother in particular, always expected me to know what she was feeling and what she expected me to do without telling me. And I thought this was natural. But my mother would expect me to know things, whether or not she spoke them—

AR: Ignorance of the law was no excuse.

AL: That's right. It's very confusing. And eventually I learned how to acquire vital and protective information without words. My mother used to say to me, "Don't just listen like a ninny to what people say in their mouth." But then she'd proceed to say something that didn't feel right to me. You always learned from observing. You have to pick things up nonverbally because people will never tell you what you're supposed to know. You have to get it for yourself: whatever it is that you need in order to survive. And if you make a mistake you get punished for it, but that's no big thing. You become strong by doing the things you need to be strong for. This is the way genuine learning takes place. That's a very difficult way to live, but it also has served me. It's been an asset as well as a liability. When I went to high school, I found out that people really thought in different ways, perceived, puzzled out, acquired information, verbally. I had such a hard time; I never studied, I literally intuited all my teachers. That's why it was so important to get a teacher who I liked or could deal with, because I never studied, I never read my assignment, and I would get all of this stuff, what they felt, what they knew, but I missed a lot of other stuff, a lot of my own original workings.

AR: When you said you never read, you meant you never read the assignments, but you *were* reading?

AL: Yes, I was constantly reading, but not things that were assigned. And if I read things that were assigned I didn't read them the way we were supposed to. Everything was like a poem, with different curves, different levels. So I always felt that the ways I took things in were different from the ways other people took them in. I used to practice trying to think.

AR: That thing those other people presumably did. Do you remember what that was like?

AL: Yes. I had an image of trying to reach something around a corner, that it was just eluding me. The image was constantly vanishing around the corner. There was an experience I had in Mexico, when I moved to Cuernavaca …

AR: This was when you were about how old?

AL: I was nineteen. When I went to Mexico I felt myself just opening up, walking on the street, seeing all these dark people and the sunlight and the heat. I was in total ecstasy. And I was also terrified. I had never lived that far from New York before. I had gone to Stamford to work in the electronics factory, but that was a little trip. From Mexico City, I moved to Cuernavaca and I met Eudora and I was commuting to Mexico City for classes. In order to get to my early class I would catch a six o'clock *turismo* in the village plaza. I would come out of my house before dawn. You know, there are two volcanoes, Popocatepetl and Ixtacuhuatl. I thought they were clouds, the first time I saw them through my windows. It would be dark, and I would see the snow on top of the mountains, and the sun coming up. And when the sun crested, at a certain point, the birds would start. But because we were in the valley it would still look like night. But there would be the light of the snow. And then this incredible crescendo of birds. One morning I came over the hill and the green, wet smells came up. And then the birds, the sound of them I'd never really noticed, never *heard* birds before. I was walking down the hill and I was transfixed. It was very beautiful. I hadn't been writing all the time I was in Mexico. And the poetry was the thing I had with words, that was so important. … And on that hill, I had the first intimation that I could bring those two together. I could infuse words directly with what I was feeling. I didn't have to create the world I wrote about. I realized that words could tell. That there was such a thing as an emotional sentence. Until then, I would make these constructs and somewhere in there would be a nugget, like a Chinese bun, there would be a piece of nourishment, the thing I really needed, which I had to create. There on that hill, I was filled with the smell and feeling and the way it looked, filled with such beauty that I could not believe—I had always fantasized it before. I used to fantasize trees and dream forest. Until I got spectacles when I was four I thought trees were green clouds. When I read Shakespeare in high school I would get off on his gardens and Spanish moss and roses and trellises with beautiful women at rest and sun on red brick. When I was in Mexico I found out this could be a reality. And I learned that day on the mountain, that words can match that, *re*-create it.

AR: Do you think that in Mexico you were seeing a reality as extraordinary and vivid and sensual as you had been fantasizing it could be?

AL: I think so. I had always thought I had to do it in my head, make it up. I learned in Mexico that you can't even make it up unless it happens, or can happen. Where it happened first for me I don't know; I do remember stories my mother would tell us about Grenada in the West Indies, where she was born ... But that morning in Mexico I realized I did not have to make beauty up for the rest of my life. I remember trying to tell Eudora about this epiphany, and I didn't have the words for it. And I remember her saying, "Write a poem." When I tried to write a poem about the way I felt that morning, I could not do it, and all I had therefore was the memory that there must be a way. And that was incredibly important. I know that I came back from Mexico very very different, and much of it had to do with what I learned from Eudora and the ways in which I loved her, but more than that, it was a kind of releasing of my work, a real releasing of myself, a connection. I think probably also that I'd passed a very crucial adolescent point.

AR: Then you went back to the Lower East Side, right?

AL: Yes, I went back to living with my friend Ruth, and I began trying to get a job. I had had a year of college, but I could not function in those people's world. So I thought I could be a nurse. And I was having such a hard time getting any kind of work, I felt, well, a practical nursing license, and then I'll go back to Mexico—

AR: With my trade.

AL: Yes. But that wasn't possible either. I didn't have any money, and black women were not given practical nursing fellowships. I didn't realize it at the time, because what they said was that my eyes were too bad. But the first thing I did when I came back was to write a piece of prose about Mexico, called "La Llorona." La Llorona is a legend in that part of Mexico, around Cuernavaca. You know Cuernavaca? You know the big *barrancas*? When the rains come to the mountains, the boulders rush through the big ravines. The sound, the first rush, would start one or two days before the rains came. All the rocks tumbling down from the mountains made a voice, and the echoes would resound and it would be a sound of weeping, with the waters behind it. Modesta, a woman who lived in the house, told me the legend of La Llorona. A woman had three sons and found her husband lying in another woman's bed—it's the Medea story—and drowned her sons in the *barrancas*, drowned her children. And every year around this time she comes back to mourn the deaths. I took this story and out of a combination of ways I was feeling I wrote a story called "La Llorona." It's a story essentially of my mother and me, it was as if I had picked my mother up and put her in that place, here is this woman who kills, who wants something, the woman who consumes her children, who wants too much, but wants not because she's evil but because she wants her own life, but by now it is so distorted … It was a very strange unfinished story, but the dynamic—

AR: It sounds like you were trying to pull those two pieces of your life together, your mother and what you'd learned in Mexico.

AL: Yes. You see, I didn't deal at all with how strong my mother was inside of me, but she was—nor with how involved I was. But this story is beautiful. Pieces of it are in my head where the poetry pool is—phrases and so on. I had never written prose before and I've never written any since until just now.

I published it under the name "Rey Domini" in a magazine …

AR: Why did you use a pseudonym?

AL: Because … I don't write stories. I write poetry. So I had to put it under another name.

AR: Because it was a different piece of you?

AL: That's right. I only write poetry and here is this story. But I used the name "Rey Domini," which is "Audre Lorde" in Latin.

AR: Did you really not write prose from the time of that story until a couple of years ago, when you wrote "Poems Are Not Luxuries"?

AL: I couldn't. For some reason, the more poetry I wrote, the less I felt I could write prose. Someone would ask for a book review, or, when I worked at the library, for a précis about books—it wasn't that I didn't have the skills. I knew about sentences by that time. I knew how to construct a paragraph. But communicating deep feeling in linear, solid blocks of print felt arcane, a method beyond me.

AR: But you'd been writing letters like wildfire, hadn't you?

AL: Well, I didn't write letters as such. I wrote stream of consciousness and for people who were close enough to me this would serve. My friends gave me back the letters I wrote them from Mexico—strange, those are the most formed. I remember feeling I could not focus on a thought long enough to have it from start to finish, but I could ponder a poem for days, camp out in its world.

AR: Do you think that was because you still had this idea that thinking was a mysterious process that other people did and that you had to sort of practice? That it wasn't something you just did?

AL: It was a very mysterious process for me. And it was one I had come to suspect, because I had seen so many errors committed in its name, and I had come not to respect it. On the other hand, I was also afraid of it, because there were inescapable conclusions or convictions I had come to about my own life, my own feelings that defied thought. And I wasn't going to let them go. I wasn't going to give them up. They were too precious to me. They were life to me. But I couldn't analyze or understand them, because they didn't make the kind of sense I had been taught to expect through understanding. There were things I knew and couldn't say, I couldn't talk about them, but I knew. And I couldn't understand them.

AR: In the sense of being able to take them out, analyze them, defend them?

AL: ... write prose about them. Right. I wrote a lot of those poems you first knew me by, those poems in *The First Cities*, way back in high school. If you had asked me to talk about one of those poems, I'd have talked in the most banal ways. All I had was the sense that I had to hold on to these things and that I had to air them in some way.

AR: But they were also being transformed into language.

AL: That's right. When I wrote something that finally had it, I would say it aloud and it would come alive, become real. It would start repeating itself and I'd know, that's struck, that's true. Like a bell. Something struck true. And there the words would be.

* * *

AR: How do you feel writing connected for you with teaching?

AL: Adrienne, I know teaching is a survival technique. It is for me, and I think it is in general; and that's the only way real teaching, real learning, happens. Because I myself was learning something I needed, to continue living. And I was examining it and teaching it at the same time I was learning it. I was teaching it to myself *aloud*. And it started out at Tougaloo in a poetry workshop.

AR: You were ill when you were called to go down to Tougaloo?

AL: Yes, I felt—I had almost died.

AR: What was going on?

AL: Diane di Prima—that was 1967—she had started the Poets Press; and she said, "You know, it's time you had a book." And I said, "Well, who's going to print it?" I was going to put those poems away, because I had found I was revising too much instead of writing new poems, and that's how I found out, again through experience, that poetry is not Play-Doh. You can't take a poem and keep re-forming it. It is itself, and you have to know how to cut it, and if there's something else you want to say, that's fine. But I was repolishing and repolishing, and Diane said, "You have to print these. Put 'em out." And the Poets Press published *The First Cities*. Well, I worked on that book, getting it together, and it was going into press … I had gotten the proofs back and I started repolishing again and realized, "This is going to be a book!" Putting myself on the line. People I don't even know are going to read these poems. What's going to happen? It felt very critical, and I was in an absolute blaze of activity, because things financially were so bad at home. And I went out and got a job, I was with the two kids in the daytime and worked at the library at night. Jonathan used to cry every night when I left, and I would hear his shrieks going down this long hall to the elevator. I was working nights, and I'd apprenticed myself to a stained-glass-window maker, and I was working in my mother's office, and making Christmas for my friends, and I became very ill—I had overdone it. I was too sick to get up, and Ed answered the phone. It was Galen Williams from the Poetry Center asking if I'd like to go as poet in residence to Tougaloo, a black college in Mississippi. I'd been recommended for a grant. It was Ed who said, "You have to do this." My energy was at such a low ebb that I couldn't see how—first of all, it was very frightening to me, the idea of someone responding to me as a poet. This book, by the way, hadn't even come out yet, you understand?

AR: And suddenly you were already being taken seriously by unseen people out there.

AL: That's right. In particular, I was asked to be public; to speak *as*, rather than *to*. But I felt as if I'd come back from the dead at that point, and so everything was up for grabs. I thought, hey, very good, let's see—not because I felt I could do it, I just knew it was new and different. I was terrified to go south. Then there were echoes of an old dream: I had wanted to go to Tougaloo years before. My friend

Elaine and I were going to join the Freedom Riders in Jackson when we left California in 1961 to return to New York, and Elaine's mother got down on her knees in San Francisco and begged us please not to do this, that they would kill us, and we didn't do it. So going to Tougaloo in Jackson was part of the mythic—

AR: But it sounds as if earlier you had been more romantic about what going south would mean, and six years later, with two kids *and* everything that had happened in between in the south—

AL: I was scared. I thought: "I'm going." Really, it was the first thing that countered the fury and pain I felt at leaving that little boy screaming every night. It was like—all right, if I can walk out and hear that child screaming in order to go down to the library and work every night, then I'm gonna be able at least to do something that I want to find out about. So I went.

AR: Were you scared at Tougaloo, in terms of teaching, meeting your first workshop?

AL: Yes, but it was a nurturing atmosphere. I'd lived there for two weeks. I went around really gathering people, and there were eight students who were already writing poetry. The ways in which I was on the line in Tougaloo … I began to learn about courage, I began to learn to talk. But this was a small group and there was a dynamic between us. We became very close. I learned so much from listening to people. And all I knew was, the only thing I had was honesty and openness. And it was absolutely necessary for me to declare, as terrified as I was, from the very get-go as soon as we were opening to each other, to say, "The father of my children is white." And what that meant in Tougaloo to those young black people then, and to deal with it, to talk about myself openly, to deal with their hostility, their sense of disillusionment, to come past that, was very hard.

AR: It must have been particularly hard since you knew by then that the marriage was going nowhere. It's like having to defend something that was not in itself defensible.

AL: What I was defending was something that needs defense. And this almost moved it out of "I'm defending Ed because I want to live with him." It was "I'm defending this relationship because we have a right to examine it and try it." So there's Audre as the northern black poet, making contact with these young southern black people who are *not* saying, "This is what we need you for," but were telling me by who they were what they needed from me. In the poem "Black Studies" a lot of that starts coming through.[3] Tougaloo laid the foundation for that poem, that knowledge born five years later. My students needed my perception, yet my perception of their need was different from what they were saying. What they were saying aloud was, "We need strong black people"—but what they were also saying was that their ideas of what strong was had come from our oppressors and didn't jibe with their feelings at all.

It was through poetry that we began to deal with these things—formally, I knew nothing. Adrienne, I had never read a book about poetry! Never read a book about poetry. I picked up one day a book by Karl Shapiro—a little thin white book. I opened it and something he said made sense. It was, "Poetry

3 Audre Lorde, *New York Head Shop and Museum* (Detroit: Broadside Press, 1974), 52–56.

doesn't make Cadillacs." That was a symbol for all the things I was—yes. So I would talk to the students, and I was learning. It was the first time I'd ever talked about writing, because always before I'd listened—part of my being inarticulate, inscrutable, because I didn't understand in terms of verbalization, and if I did I was too terrified to speak anyway. But at Tougaloo *we* talked about poetry. And I got the first copies of my book there at Tougaloo. I had never been in this relationship with black people before. Never. There had been a very uneasy dialogue between me and the Harlem Writers' Guild, where I felt I was tolerated but never really accepted—that I was both crazy and queer but would grow out of it all. Johnny Clarke adopted me because he really loved me, and he's a kind man, you know? And he taught me wonderful things about Africa. And he said to me, "You are a poet. You *are* a poet. I don't understand your poetry but you are a poet, you are." So I would get this underlining of me. "You're not doing what you're supposed to do, but, yes, you can do it and we totally expect you to. You are a bright and shining light. You're off on a lot of wrong turns, women, the Village, white people, all of this, but you're young yet. You'll find your way." So I would get these double messages. This kind of underlining and rejection at the same time—it reduplicated my family, you see. In my family it was: "You're a Lorde, so that makes you special and particular above anybody else in the world. But you're not our kind of Lorde, so when are you going to straighten up and act right?"

AR: And did you feel, there in the Harlem Writers' Guild, the same kind of unwritten laws that you had to figure out in order to do right?

AL: Yes, I would bring poems to read at the meetings. And hoping, well, they're gonna tell me actually what it is they want, but they never could, never did.

AR: Were there women in that group, older women?

AL: Rosa Guy was older than I, but she was still very young. I remember only one other woman, Gertrude McBride. But she came in and out of the workshop so quickly I never knew her. For the most part the men were the core. My friend Jeannie and I were members but in a slightly different position, we were in high school, you see.

AR: And so Tougaloo was an entirely different experience of working with other black writers.

AL: When I went to Tougaloo, I didn't know what to give or where it was going to come from. I knew I couldn't give what regular teachers of poetry give, nor did I want to, because they'd never served me. I couldn't give what English teachers give. The only thing I had to give was me. And I was so involved with these young people—I really loved them. I knew the emotional life of each of those students because we would have conferences, and that became inseparable from their poetry. And I would talk to them in the group about their poetry in terms of what I knew about their lives, and that there was a real connection between the two that was inseparable no matter what they'd been taught to the contrary.

I knew by the time I left Tougaloo that teaching was the work I needed to be doing, that library work—by this time I was head librarian at the Town School—being a librarian was not enough. It had been very satisfying to me. And I had a kind of stature I hadn't had before in terms of working. But from the time I went to Tougaloo and did that workshop, I knew: not only, yes, I am a poet, but also, this is the kind of work I'm going to do.

Practically all the poems in *Cables to Rage* I wrote in Tougaloo.[4] I was there for six weeks. I came back knowing that my relationship with Ed was not enough: either we were going to change it or end it. I didn't know how to end it, because there had never been any endings for me. But I had met Frances at Tougaloo, and I knew she was going to be a permanent person in my life. However, I didn't know how we were going to work it out. I'd left a piece of my heart in Tougaloo not just because of Frances but because of what my students there had taught me.

And I came back, and my students called me and said—they were all of them also in the Tougaloo choir—they were coming to New York to sing in Carnegie Hall with Duke Ellington on April 4, and I covered it for the *Clarion-Ledger*, in Jackson, so I was there, and while we were there Martin Luther King was killed.

AR: On that night?

AL: I was with the Tougaloo choir at Carnegie Hall when he was killed. They were singing "What the World Needs Now Is Love." And they interrupted it to tell us that Martin Luther King had been killed.

AR: What did people do?

AL: Duke Ellington started to cry. Honeywell, the head of the choir, said, "The only thing we can do here is finish this as a memorial." And they sang again, "What the World Needs Now Is Love." The kids were crying. The audience was crying. And then the choir stopped. They cut the rest of it short. But

4 Audre Lorde, *Cables to Rage* (London: Paul Breman, Heritage Series, 1970).

they sang that song and it kept reverberating. It was more than pain. The horror, the enormity of what was happening. Not just the death of King, but what it meant. I have always had the sense of Armageddon and it was much stronger in those days, the sense of living on the edge of chaos. Not just personally, but on the world level. That we were dying, that we were killing our world—that sense had always been with me. That whatever I was doing, whatever we were doing that was creative and right, functioned to hold us from going over the edge. That this was the most we could do, while we constructed some saner future. But that we were in that kind of peril. And here it was reality, in fact. Some of the poems—"Equinox" is one of them—come from then. I knew then that I had to leave the library. And it was just about this time that Yolanda took my book, *The First Cities*, to Mina Shaughnessy who had been her teacher, and I think she said to Mina, "Why don't you have her teach?"— because that's the way, you know, Yolanda is.[5,6]

AR: But also, Mina would have listened to that.

AL: So Yolanda came home and said, "Hey, the head of the SEEK English program wants to meet you.[7] Maybe you can get a job there." And I thought, I have to lay myself on the line.[7] It's not going back south and being shot at, but when Mina said to me, "Teach," it was as threatening as that was. I felt at the time, I don't know how I'm gonna do it, but that's the

5 Audre Lorde, *The First Cities* (New York: Poets Press, 1968).
6 Mina Shaughnessy (1924–78), then director of the SEEK Writing Program at the City College, City University of New York.
7 "Search for Education, Elevation, and Knowledge": A prebaccalaureate program in compensatory education in the City University of New York in which a number of writer-teachers participated in the 1960s and early 1970s.

front line for me. And I talked to Frances about this, because we'd had the Tougaloo experience, and I said, "If I could go to war, if I could pick up a gun to defend the things I believe, yes—but what am I gonna do in a classroom?" And Frances said, "You'll do just what you did at Tougaloo." And the first thing that I said to my SEEK students was, "I'm scared too."

AR: I know *I* went in there in terror. But I went in white terror: you know: now you're on the line, all your racism is going to show …

AL: I went in, in Audre terror, black terror. I thought, I have responsibility to these students. How am I going to speak to them? How am I going to tell them what I want from them—literally, that kind of terror. I did not know how to open my mouth and be understood. And my *commadre*, Yolanda, who was also a student in the SEEK program, said, "I guess you're just going to have to talk to them the same way you talk to me because I'm one of them and you've gotten across to me." I learned every single thing in every classroom. Every single class I ever walked into was like doing it anew. Every day, every week; but that was the exciting thing.

AR: Did you teach English 1—that back-to-back course where you could be a poet—a writing teacher—and not teach grammar, and they had an English instructor to teach the grammar? That was the only way I could have started doing it either.

AL: I learned to teach grammar. And then I realized that we can't separate these two things. We have to do them together because they're integral. That's when I learned how important grammar is, that part of the understanding process is grammatical. That's how I taught myself to write prose. I kept learning and learning. I'd come into my class and say, "Guess what I found out last night. Tenses are a way of ordering the chaos around time." About grammar I learned that it was arbitrary, that it served a purpose, that it helped to form the ways we thought, that it could be freeing as well as restrictive. And I sensed again how as children we learn this, and why; it's like driving a car, once we know it we can choose to discard it or use it, but you can't know if it has useful or destructive power until you have a handle on it. It's like fear, once you put your hand on it you can use it or push it away. I was saying these things in class and dealing with what was happening with Frances and me, what was going on with this insane man I lived with who wanted to continue pretending life could be looked at one way and lived another. All this, every bit of it funneling into that class. My children were just learning to read in school, and that was important too, because I could watch their processes. Then it got even heavier when I went up to Lehmann College and was teaching a class on racism in education, teaching these white students how it was, the connections between their lives and the fury …

AR: You taught a course on racism for white students at Lehmann?

AL: They were inaugurating a program in the education department, for these white kids going into teaching in the New York City schools. Lehmann used to be 99 percent white, and it was these students coming out of the education department who were going to teach black children in the city schools. So the course was called "Race and the Urban Situation." I had all these white students, wanting to know, "What are we doing? Why are our kids hating us in the classroom?" I could not believe that they did not know the most elementary level of interactions.

I would say, "When a white kid says 2 + 2 = 4, you say 'right.' In the same class, when a black kid stands up and says 2 + 2 = 4, you pat him on the back, you say, 'Hey, that's wonderful.' But what message are you really giving? Or what happens when you walk down the street on your way to teach? When you walk into class? Let's playact a little." And all the fear and loathing of these young white college students would come pouring out; it had never been addressed.

AR: They must have been mostly women, weren't they? In the education department?

AL: Yes, mostly women, and they felt like unwilling sacrifices. But I began to feel by the end of two terms that there ought to be somebody white doing this. It was terribly costly emotionally. I didn't have more than one or two black students in my class. One of them dropped out saying this wasn't right for him, and I thought, wait a minute, racism doesn't just distort white people—what about us? What about the effects of white racism upon the ways black people view each other? Racism internalized? What about black teachers going into ghetto schools? And I saw there were different problems, that were just as severe, for a black teacher going into New York City schools after a racist, sexist education.

AR: You mean in terms of expectations?

AL: Not just in terms of expectations, but of self-image, in terms of confusion about loyalties. In terms of identifying with the oppressor. And I thought, who is going to start to deal with that? What do you do about it, Audre? This was where I wanted to use my energies. Meanwhile, this is 1969, and I'm thinking, what is my place in all this? There were two black women in the class, and I tried to talk to them about us, as black women, having to get together. The black organizations on the campuses were revving up for the spring actions. And the women said, you are insane, our men need us. It was a total rejection. "No, we can't come together as women. We're black." But I had to keep trying to straighten out the threads, because I knew the minute I stopped trying to straighten this shit out it was going to engulf me. So the only hope I had was to work at it, work on all the threads. My love with Frances, Ed, the children, teaching black students, the women.

And in '69 came the black and Puerto Rican occupation at City College. I was dealing with the black students outside of class on the barricades, Yolanda and I would bring over soup and blankets, and see black women getting fucked on tables and under desks—see what went down in those occupied buildings. And meanwhile we'd be trying to speak to them as women, and all we'd hear is, "The revolution is here, right?" Seeing how black women were being used and abused was painful—putting those things together. I said, I want to teach black students again. I went to John Jay College and discussed a course with the dean on racism and the urban situation, and he said, Come teach it. I taught two courses, that one and another new course I introduced to the English department, remedial writing through creative writing. It was confrontation teaching.

AR: John Jay was largely a police college, right?

AL: It had been a police college, but I began in 1970, after open admissions started, and John Jay was now a four-year senior college with a regular enrollment as well as an enrollment of City uniformed personnel. There were no black teachers in English or history. Most of our incoming freshmen were black or Puerto Rican. And my demeanor was very unthreatening.

AR: —I've seen your demeanor at John Jay and it was not unthreatening, but that was a bit later—

AL: —and also, I was a black *woman*. So then I came in and started this course and really meant business. And it was very heavily attended. A lot of black and white policemen registered for it. And literally, I used to be terrified about the guns.

AR: They were wearing guns?

AL: Yes. And since open admissions made college accessible to all high school graduates, we had cops and kids off the block in the same class. In 1970, the Black Panthers were being murdered in Chicago. Here we had black and white cops, and black and white kids off the block. Most of the women were young, black, together women who had come to college now because they'd not been able to get in before. Some of them were SEEK students, but not all, and this was the one chance for them. A lot of them were older; they were very street wise but they had done very little work with themselves as black women, as black people. They'd done it only in relation to, against, whitey. The enemy was always outside. I did that course in the same way I did all the others, which was learning as I went along, asking the hard questions, not knowing what was coming next. Very good things happened in the classes. I wish I had recorded some of it. Like the young white cop in the class saying, "Yeah, but everybody needs someone to look down on, don't they?" By then I'd learned how to talk. In my own fashion. Things weren't all concise or refined, but enough of it got through to them, their own processes would start. I came to realize that in one term that is the most you can do. There are people who can give chunks of information, perhaps, but that was not what I was about. The learning process is something you can incite, literally incite, like a riot. And then, just possibly, hopefully, it goes home, or on.

By that time the battle over the Black Studies Department had started at John Jay. And again I saw the use and abuse of women, of black people, saw how black studies was being used by the university in a really cynical fashion. A year later, I returned to the English Department. I had made a number of enemies. One of the attempts to discredit me among black students was to say I was a lesbian. Now by this time, I would have considered myself uncloseted, but I had never discussed my own poetry at John Jay, nor my sexuality. I knew, as I had always known, that the only way you can head people off from using who you are against you is to be honest and open first, to talk about yourself before they talk about you. It wasn't even courage. Speaking up was a protective mechanism for myself—like publishing "Love Poem" in *MS. Magazine* in 1971 and bringing it in and putting it up on the wall of the English Department.

AR: I remember hearing you read "Love Poem" on the Upper West Side, a coffeehouse at 72nd Street. It was the first time I'd heard you read it. And I think it was about that time, the early seventies. You read it. It was incredible. Like defiance. It was glorious.

AL: That's how I was feeling. I was always feeling my back against the wall, because, as bad as it is now, the idea of open lesbianism in the black community was—I mean, we've moved miles in a very short time. But in the early seventies it was totally horrible. My publisher called and literally said he didn't understand the words of "Love Poem." He said, "Now what is this all about, are you supposed to be a man?" And he was a poet! And I said, "No, I'm loving a woman."

AR: Well, don't tell me that your publisher had never heard of lesbians.

AL: I'm sure he had, but the idea that *I'd* write a poem—

AR: —That one of his poets in the Broadside Series—

AL: That's right. And he was a sensitive man. He was a poet.

AR: But he did print your work.

AL: Yes, he did. But he didn't print that poem, the first time around. "Love Poem" was supposed to have been in *From a Land Where Other People Live*.[8]

AR: And it wasn't published in that book? You took it out?

AL: Yes. He didn't want it. There was another—was it "American Cancer Society"?—that belonged in *From a Land*. But when you heard me read "Love Poem," I had already made up my mind that I wasn't going to be worrying anymore over who knows and who doesn't know that I have always loved women. One thing has always kept me going—and it's not

8 Audre Lorde, *From a Land Where Other People Live* (Detroit: Broadside Press, 1973).

really courage or bravery, unless that's what courage or bravery is made up of—is a sense that there are so many ways in which I'm vulnerable and cannot help but be vulnerable, I'm not going to be vulnerable by putting weapons of silence in my enemies' hands. Being a lesbian in the black community, or even being woman-identified, is difficult and dangerous.

When a people share a common oppression, certain kinds of skills and joint defenses are developed. And if you survive you survive because those skills and defenses have worked. When you come into conflict over other existing differences, there already is an additional vulnerability to each other which is desperate and very deep. And that is, for example, what happens between black men and women, because we have certain weapons we have perfected together that white women and men have not shared. I said this to someone, and she said, very rightly, the same thing exists within the Jewish community between Jewish men and Jewish women. I think the oppression is different, therefore the need for connection is on a different level, but the same mechanism of vulnerability exists. When you share a common oppression you have certain additional weapons against each other, because you've forged them in secret together against a common enemy. It's a fear that I'm still not free of and that I remember all the time when I deal with other black women: the fear of the excomrade.

* * *

AR: In "Poems Are Not Luxuries," you wrote: "The white fathers told us, 'I think therefore I am,' and the black mothers in each of us—the poets—whisper in our dreams, 'I feel therefore I can be free.'" I've heard it remarked that here you are simply restating the old stereotype of the rational white male and the emotional dark female. I believe you were saying something very different, but could you talk a little about that?

AL: There are a couple of things. I have heard that accusation, that I'm contributing to the stereotype, that I'm saying the province of intelligence and rationality belongs to the white male. But that is like—if you're traveling a road that begins nowhere and ends nowhere, the ownership of that road is meaningless. If you have no land out of which the road comes, no place that road goes to, geographically, no goal, then the existence of that road is totally meaningless. So leaving rationality to the white man is like leaving to him a piece of that road that begins nowhere and ends nowhere. When I talk about the black mothers in each of us, the poets, I don't mean the black mothers in each of us who are called poets, I mean the black mother—

AR: Who *is* the poet?

AL: The black mother who is the poet in every one of us. Now when males, or patriarchal thinking whether it's male or female, reject that combination then we're truncated. Rationality is not unnecessary. It serves the chaos of knowledge. It serves feeling. It serves to get from some place to some place. If you don't honor those places then the road is meaningless. Too often, that's what happens with intellect and rationality and that circular, academic, analytic thinking. But ultimately, I don't see feel/think as a dichotomy. I see them as a choice of ways and combinations.

AR: Which we are constantly making. We don't make it once and for all. We constantly have to be making it, depending on where we are, over and over.

AL: But I do think that we have been taught to think,

to codify information in certain old ways, to learn, to understand in certain ways. The possible shapes of what has not been before exist only in that back place, where we keep those unnamed, untamed longings for something different and beyond what is now called possible, to which our analysis and our understanding can only build roads. But we have been taught to deny those fruitful areas of ourselves which exist in every human being. I personally believe that those black mothers exist more in women; yet that is the name for a humanity that men are not without. But they have taken a position against that piece of themselves, and it is a world position, a position throughout time. And I've said this to you before, Adrienne, I feel that we're evolving. In terms of a species—

AR: That women are evolving—

AL: Yes, that the human race is evolving through women. That it's not by accident that there are more and more women, the—this sounds crazy, doesn't it—the production of women, women being born, women surviving ... And we've got to take that promise of new power seriously, or we'll make the same mistakes all over again. Unless we learn the lessons of the black mothers in each of us, whether we are black or not—I believe this exists in men also but they choose to eschew it, not to deal with it. Which is, as I learned, their right of choice. Hopefully this choice can be affected, but I don't know. I don't believe this shift from conquering problems to experiencing life is a one-generational shot or a single investment. I believe it's a whole signature which you try to set in motion and have some input into. But I'm not saying that women don't think or analyze.
Or that white does not feel. I'm saying that we must amalgamate the two, never close our eyes to the terror, the chaos which is black which is creative

which is female which is dark which is rejected which is messy which is—

AR: Sinister—

AL: Sinister, smelly, erotic, confused, upsetting—

AR: I think we have to keep using and affirming a vocabulary that has been used negatively and pejoratively. And I assume that's the statement you're making in that sentence, that you make over and over in your poetry. And it's nothing as simplistic as saying "black is beautiful," either.

AL: There's nothing beautiful about a black machine. You know, Adrienne, when I was in high school, I was trying to get a poem about love published in the school magazine. The editor of the magazine was named Renee—she was very intelligent, very grown-up, very beautiful. And Renee said to me, softening her rejection of my poem, "After all, Audre, you don't want to be a sensualist poet." That, obviously, was something you're not supposed to be.

AR: I was told, as a poet, you're not supposed to be angry, you're not supposed to be personal.

AL: After I published "Uses of the Erotic," a number of women who read it said that this is antifeminist, that the use of the erotic as a guide is—

AR: Antifeminist?

AL: Is reducing us once again to the unseen, the unusable. That in writing it I am returning us to a place of total intuition without insight.

AR: And yet, in that essay you're talking about work

and power—about two of the most political things that exist.

AL: Yes, but what they see is—and I address this at the very beginning: I try to say that the erotic has been used against us, even the word itself, so often, that we have been taught to suspect what is deepest in ourselves, and that is the way we learn to testify against ourselves, against our feelings. When we talk about racism or nationalism we can see it. When we're talking in terms of our lives and survival as women, we don't. The way you get people to testify against themselves is not constantly to have police tactics and oppressive techniques. What you do is to build it in, so people learn to distrust everything in themselves that has not been sanctioned, to reject what is most creative in themselves—to have *them* reject it to begin with, so you don't even need to stamp it out. A black woman devaluating another black woman's work. The black women buying that hot comb and putting it in my locker at the library. It wasn't even black men, it was black women testifying against ourselves. This turning away from the erotic on the part of some of our best minds, our most creative and analytic women, is disturbing and destructive, and should be countered. Because we cannot fight old power in old power terms. The only way we can do it is by creating another whole structure that touches every aspect of our existence.

AR: And as you were saying about courses, black studies, women's studies: this is not just a question of being "allowed" to have our history or literature or theory in the old power framework. It is every minute of our lives, from our dreams to getting up and brushing our teeth to when we go to teach—

AL: There are different choices facing black and white women in life, certain specifically different pitfalls surrounding us because of our experiences, our color. Not only are some of the problems that face us dissimilar, but some of the entrapments and the weapons used to neutralize us are not the same. For instance, being used against another oppressed group is not something that exists for white women in the same way as it does for black women. It's very easy for black women to be used against black men, not because they're men but because they're black. And we have to be able to separate the oppressor's needs from our legitimate conflict of interests at any time. Another example, for white women, is the pitfall of being invited to join the oppressor in his oppressing.

AR: The invitation to inclusion …

AL: Yes. The apparent invitation to power. It's not something that exists on a real level for black women. The closest face is tokenism, but that is not an invitation to power. We are never invited to join the real power, that's understood, simply because we *are* black, and that would mean having to accommodate visible, constant difference. White women can be more easily ignored, assimilated, or explained away.

AR: I wish we could explore this more—about you and me, but also in general. I think it needs to be talked about, written about: the differences in alternatives or choices we are offered as black and white women. There is a danger of seeing it in an all-or-nothing way. I think it's a very complex thing. White women are constantly offered choices, or the appearance of choices. But also real choices that are undeniable. We don't always perceive the difference between the two.

AL: Adrienne, in my journals I have a lot of pieces of conversations that I'm having with you in my head. I'll be having a conversation with you and I'll put it in my journal because stereotypically or symbolically these conversations occur in a space of black woman/ white woman, where it's beyond Adrienne and Audre, almost as if we're two voices.

AR: You mean the conversations you have in your head and your journal, or the conversations we're having on this earth?

AL: The conversations that exist in my head that I put in the journal. This piece, I think, is one of them—about the different pitfalls. I've never forgotten the impatience in your voice that time on the telephone—when you said, "It's not enough to say to me that you intuit it." Do you remember? I will never forget that. Even at the same time that I understood what you meant, I felt a total wipeout of my modus, my way of perceiving and formulating.

AR: Yes, but it's not a wipeout of your modus. Because I don't think my modus is unintuitive, right? And one of the crosses I've borne all my life is being told that I'm rational, logical, cool—I am not cool, and I'm not rational and logical in that icy sense. But there's a way in which, trying to translate from your experience to mine, I do need to hear chapter and verse from time to time. I'm afraid of it all slipping away into: "Ah, yes, I understand you." You remember, that telephone conversation was in connection with the essay I was writing on feminism and racism. I was trying to say to you, don't let's let this evolve into "You don't understand me" or "I can't understand you" or "Yes, of course we understand each other because we love each other." That's bullshit. So if I ask for documentation, it's because I take seriously the spaces between us that difference has created, that racism has created. There are times when I simply cannot assume that I know what you know, unless you show me what you mean.

AL: But I'm used to associating a *request* for documentation as a questioning of my perceptions, an attempt to devalue what I'm in the process of discovering.

AR: It's not. Help me to perceive what you perceive. That's what I'm trying to say to you.

AL: But documentation does not help one perceive, at best it only analyzes the perception. At worst, it provides a screen by which to avoid concentrating on the core revelation, following it down to how it feels. Again, knowledge and understanding. They can function in concert, but they don't replace each other. But I'm not rejecting your need for documentation.

AR: And in fact, I feel you've been giving it to me, in your poems always, and most recently in the long prose piece you've been writing, and in talks we've been having. I don't feel the absence of it now.

AL: Don't forget I'm a librarian. I became a librarian because I really believed I would gain tools for ordering and analyzing information. I couldn't know everything in the world, but I thought I would gain tools for learning it. But that was of limited value. I can document the road to Abomey for you, and true, you might not get there without that information. I can respect what you're saying. But once you get there, only you know why, what you came for, as you search for it and perhaps find it.

So at certain stages that request for documentation is a blinder, a questioning of my perceptions.

Someone once said to me that I hadn't documented the goddess in Africa, the woman bond that moves throughout *The Black Unicorn*. I had to laugh. I told her, "I'm a poet, not a historian. I've shared my knowledge, I hope. Now you go document it, if you wish."

I don't know about you, Adrienne, but I have a difficult enough time making my perceptions verbal, tapping that deep place, forming that handle, and documentation at that point is often useless. Perceptions precede analysis just as visions precede action or accomplishments. It's like getting a poem—

That's the only thing I have to fight with, my whole life, preserving my perceptions of how things are, and later, learning to accept and correct both at the same time, and doing this in the face of tremendous opposition and cruel judgment. And I spent a long period of time questioning my perceptions and my first interior knowledge, not dealing with them, being tripped by them.

AR: Well, I think that there's another element in all this between us. Certainly in that particular conversation on the telephone where I said, you have to tell me chapter and verse. I've had great resistance to some of your perceptions. They can be very painful to me. Perceptions about what goes on between us, what goes on between black and white people, what goes on between black and white women. So, it's not that I can just accept your perceptions unblinkingly. Some of them are very hard for me. But I don't want to deny them. I know I can't afford to. I may have to take a long hard look and say, Is this something I can use? What do I do with this?—try to stand back and not become immersed in what you so forcefully are pronouncing. So there's a piece of me that wants to resist wholly, and a piece that wants to accept wholly, and there's some place in between where I have to find my own ground. What I can't afford is either to wipe out your perceptions, or to pretend I understand you when I don't. And then, if it's a question of racism—and I don't mean just the overt violence out there but also all the differences in our ways of seeing—there's always the question: How do I use this? What do I do about it?

AL: "How much of this truth can I bear to see / and still live / unblinded? How much of this pain / can I use?"[9] What holds us all back is being unable to ask that crucial question, that essential step deflected. You know the piece I wrote for *The Black Scholar*?[10] The piece was useful, but limitedly so because I didn't ask some essential question. And not having asked myself that question, not having realized that it *was* a question, I was deflecting a lot of energy in that piece. I kept reading it over, thinking, this isn't quite what it should be. I thought at the time I was holding back because it would be totally unacceptable in *The Black Scholar*. That wasn't it really. I was holding back because I had not asked *myself* the question: Why is women loving women so threatening to black men, unless they want to assume the white male position? It was a question of how much I could bear, and of not realizing I could bear more than I thought I could at the time. It was also a question of how could I use that perception other than just in rage or destruction.

9 Audre Lord, "Need," in *Heresies: a feminist publication* 2, no. 4 (1979): 112–13.
10 Audre Lorde, "Scratching the Surface: Some Notes on Barriers to Women and Loving," in *Black Scholar* 9, no. 7 (1978): 31–36.

AR: Speaking of rage and destruction, what do you really mean by the first five lines of "Power"?[11]

AL: "The difference between poetry / and rhetoric / is being / ready to kill yourself / instead of your children." What was I feeling? I was very involved in a case—

AR: The white policeman who shot the black child and was acquitted. We had lunch around the time you were writing that poem and you were full of it.

AL: I was driving in the car, and heard the news on the radio—that the cop had been acquitted. I was really sickened with fury, and I decided to pull over and just jot some things down in my notebook to enable me to cross town without an accident, to continue functioning because I felt so sick and so enraged. And I wrote those lines down—I was just writing, and that poem came out without craft, that's probably why I was talking to you about it, because I didn't feel it was really a poem. I was thinking that the killer had been a student at John Jay and that I might have seen him in the hall, that I might see him again. What was retribution? What could have been done? There was one black woman on the jury. It could have been me. Now I am here teaching in John Jay College. Do I kill him? What is my effective role? Would I kill her in the same way—the black woman on the jury. What kind of strength did she, would I, have at the point of deciding to take a position—

AR: Against eleven white men …

11 In Audre Lorde, *The Black Unicorn* (New York: W. W. Norton & Co., 1978), 108–10.

AL: … That archaic fear of the total reality of a power that is not on your terms. There is the jury, white male power, white male structures, how do you take a position against them? How do you reach down into threatening difference without being killed or killing? How do you deal with things you believe, live them not as theory, not even as emotion, but right on the line of action and effect and change? All of those things were riding in on that poem. But I had no sense, no understanding at the time, of the connections, just that I *was* that woman. And that to put myself on the line to do what had to be done at any place and time was so difficult, yet absolutely crucial, and not to do so was the most awful death. And putting yourself on the line is like killing a piece of yourself, in the sense that you have to kill, end, destroy something familiar and dependable, so that something new can come, in ourselves, in our world. And that sense of writing at the edge, out of urgency, not because you choose it but because you have to, that sense of survival—that's what the poem is out of, as well as the pain of my son's death over and over. Once you live any piece of your vision it opens you to a constant onslaught. Of necessities, of horrors, but of wonders too, of possibilities.

AR: I was going to say, tell it on the other side.

AL: Of wonders, absolute wonders, possibilities, like meteor showers all the time, bombardment, constant connections. And then, trying to separate what is useful for survival from what is distorted, destructive to self.

AR: There's so much with which that has to be done —rejecting the distortions, keeping what we can use. Even in work created by people we admire intensely.

AL: Yes, a commitment to being selectively open. I had to do that with my physical survival. How am I going to live with cancer and not succumb to it in the many ways that I could? What do I have to do? And coming up against: There's no one to tell you even possibilities. In the hospital I kept thinking, let's see, there's got to be someone somewhere, a black lesbian feminist with cancer, how'd she handle it? Then I realized, hey, honey, you are *it*, for now. I read all of those books and then I realized, no one can tell me how to do it. I have to pick and choose, see what feels right. Determination, poetry—well that's all in the work.

AR: I'm thinking about when you had just had the first biopsy, in 1977, and we were both supposed to speak on a panel in Chicago. On "The Transformation of Silence into Language and Action." And you said there was no way you were going to the MLA—remember? That you couldn't do it, you didn't need to do it, that doing it could not mean anything important to you. But in fact you went out there and said what you said, and it was for yourself but not only for yourself.[12]

AL: You said, why don't you tell them about what you've just been through? That's what you said. And I started saying, now that doesn't have anything to do with the panel. And as I said that I felt the words "silence." "Transformation." I hadn't spoken about this experience …

This is silence … Can I transform this? Is there any connection? Most of all, how do I share it? And that's how a setting down became clear on paper, as if the connections became clear in the setting down. That paper and "A Litany for Survival" came about at the

12 See "The Transformation of Silence into Language and Action," in *Sinister Wisdom*, vol. 6 (1978), 11–15.

same time. I had the feeling, probably a body sense, that life was never going to be the same. If not now, eventually, this was something I would have to face, if not cancer, then somehow, I would have to examine the terms and means as well as the whys of my survival—and in the face of alteration.[13] So much of the work I did, I did before I knew consciously that I had cancer. Questions of death and dying, dealing with power and strength, the sense of "What am I paying for?" that I wrote about in that paper, were crucial to me a year later. "Uses of the Erotic" was written four weeks before I found out I had breast cancer, in 1978.

AR: Again, it's like what you were saying before, about making the poems that didn't exist, that you needed to have exist.

AL: The existence of that paper enabled me to pick up and go to Houston and California, it enabled me to start working again. I don't know when I'd have been able to write again, if I hadn't had those words. Do you realize, we've come full circle, because that is where knowing and understanding mesh. What understanding begins to do is to make knowledge available for use, and that's the urgency, that's the push, that's the drive. I don't know how I wrote the long prose piece I have just finished, but I just knew that I had to do it.

AR: That you had to understand what you knew and also make it available to others?

AL: That's right. Inseparable process now. But for me, I had to know I knew it first—I had to feel.

13 Lorde, *The Black Unicorn*, 31.

Texts:
Basma Alsharif, Erika Balsom, CAConrad, Adam Christensen, Beatrice Gibson, Gobert Glück, Mason Leaver-Yap, Ursula K. Le Guin, Audre Lorde, Eileen Myles, Alice Notley, Pauline Oliveros, Irene Revell, Adrienne Rich, Gertrude Stein, Axel Wieder.

Alice Notley, "Doctor Williams' Heiresses," published by Tuumba Press, copyright 1980 by Alice Notley, reprinted with kind permission by the author.

Eileen Myles, "Painted Clear, Painted Black," from *Evening Will Come: A Monthly Journal of Poetics* no. 29 (May 2013), reprinted with kind permission by the author.

Robert Glück, "Sanchez and Day," from *Elements of a Coffee Service* by Robert Glück, published by Grey Fox Press, copyright 1982 by Robert Glück, reprinted with kind permission by the author.

Ursula K. Le Guin, "The Fisherwoman's Daughter," from *Dancing at the Edge of the World* by Ursula K. Le Guin, copyright 1989 by Ursula K. Le Guin, reprinted the permission of Grove Atlantic, Inc.

Audre Lorde, "Uses of the Erotic: The Erotic as Power," from *Sister Outsider: Essays and Speeches* by Audre Lorde, published by Crossing Press, copyright 1984, 2007 by Audre Lorde, reprinted with the permission of the Charlotte Sheedy Literary Agency.

Adrienne Rich, "Anger and Tenderness," from *Of Woman Born: Motherhood as Experience and Institution* by Adrienne Rich, copyright 1986, 1976 by W. W. Norton & Company, Inc., reprinted with the permission of W. W. Norton & Company, Inc.

Adrienne Rich and Audre Lord, interview from *Signs* vol. 6, no. 4 (Summer 1981), pp. 713–36, reprinted with the permission of University of Chicago Press Journals.

Pauline Oliveros, "Sonic Meditations," from *Sonic Meditations* by Pauline Oliveros, Smith Publications, 1971, reprinted with the permission of The Pauline Oliveros Trust and The Ministry of Maåt.

Films:
I Hope I'm Loud When I'm Dead is commissioned by Bergen Kunsthall, KW Institute for Contemporary Art, Berlin; Camden Art Centre, London; and Mercer Union, Toronto; with support from Julia Stoschek Collection, Outset Germany_Switzerland and Arts Council Norway.

Deux Soeurs Qui Ne Sont Pas Soeurs is commissioned by Bergen Kunsthall, Borealis—a festival for experimental music, Camden Art Centre, London; and Mercer Union, Toronto; with support from Fluxus Art Projects, Arts Council England, and The Beatrice Gibson Producers Circle. The score was produced by Laurence Crane and commissioned with support from Arts Council Norway.

Published by Bergen Kunsthall and
Sternberg Press in collaboration
with KW Institute for Contemporary Art
on the occasion of the exhibitions:

Beatrice Gibson
KW Production Series
Julia Stoschek Collection, Berlin
Curated by Mason Leaver-Yap
September 27–December 16, 2018

Beatrice Gibson
Crone Music
Camden Art Centre, London
Curated by Martin Clark and Sophie Williamson
January 18–March 31, 2019

Beatrice Gibson
I Couldn't Sleep in My Dream
Bergen Kunsthall
Curated by Steinar Sekkingstad and Axel Wieder
January 25–March 31, 2019

Beatrice Gibson
Plural Dreams of Social Life
Mercer Union, a centre for contemporary art, Toronto
Curated by Julia Paoli
April 13–June 1, 2019

Editors: Beatrice Gibson, Axel Wieder
Copy editing and transcription: Jasmine Hinks
Proofreading: Jasmine Hinks, Ames Gerould
Design: HIT
Printing: Spree Druck, Berlin

ISBN 978-3-95679-546-6

Sternberg Press
Caroline Schneider
Karl-Marx-Allee 78
10243 Berlin, Germany
www.sternberg-press.com

Bergen Kunsthall
Rasmus Meyers allé 5
5015 Bergen, Norway
www.kunsthall.no

Published in collaboration with:
KW Institute for Contemporary Art
Auguststraße 69
10117 Berlin, Germany
www.kw-berlin.de

SternbergPress

BERGEN KUNSTHALL

KW

Camden Art Centre
Arkwright Road
London NW3

Mercer Union
a centre for contemporary art

Thank you

Basma Alsharif
Erika Balsom
Adam Christensen
CAConrad
Martin Clark
Ames Gerould
Robert Glück
Krist Gruijthuijsen
Lina Grumm
Tatjana Günthner
Sofia Marie Hamnes
Ragna Haugstad
Jasmine Hinks
Mai Lahn-Johannessen
Mason Leaver-Yap
Annette Lux
Peter Meanwell
Eileen Myles
Alice Notley
Julia Paoli
Hilde Marie Pedersen
Irene Revell
Eva Rowson
Tine Rude
Maria Rusinovskaya
Caroline Schneider
Steinar Sekkingstad
Jonas Skarmark
Einride Torvik
Sophie Williamson
Maja Zahl
Stein-Inge Århus